This Girl,

A series of 35 articles written by

J. Howard Wert

originally published in the

Harrisburg, Pennsylvania Patriot

from November 18, 1912 to July 14, 1913

THE
MAKING OF AMERICA
SERIES

HARRISBURG'S
OLD EIGHTH WARD

MICHAEL BARTON AND JESSICA DORMAN

Steve's favorite picture of HBC. P. 31

He will have made into a shirt P. 30

P. 118

ARCADIA

Published by Arcadia Publishing,
an imprint of Tempus Publishing, Inc.
2 Cumberland Street
Charleston, SC 29401

Printed in Great Britain.

Library of Congress Catalog Card Number: 2002104255

For all general information contact Arcadia Publishing at:
Telephone 843-853-2070
Fax 843-853-0044
E-Mail sales@arcadiapublishing.com

For customer service and orders:
Toll-Free 1-888-313-2665

Visit us on the Internet at http://www.arcadiapublishing.com

FRONT COVER: *This overview of the Eighth Ward keenly emphasizes its contrast with the new state capitol, completed in 1904. The photograph was identified as "View of district to be taken by state of Pennsylvania for enlargement of the Capitol Park. Looking from Pennsylvania Railroad." Wert calls the Old Eighth a "strenuous place on a Saturday night," with its "inevitable riot call" to police. (Historical Society of Dauphin County [HSDC])*

CONTENTS

Christie's Court was the shortest, narrowest alley in the Eighth Ward, branching southward off Cranberry Alley. Yet, there were six addresses on it. J. Howard Wert complained that every square foot of land in the neighborhood was built on. (HSDC)

ACKNOWLEDGMENTS

We owe the revival of J. Howard Wert's writings, originally titled "Passing of the Old Eighth," to several helpful institutions and individuals. At the Historical Society of Dauphin County (HSDC), in Harrisburg, Pennsylvania, it was Peter Seibert, Warren Wirebach, and Robert Hill who first pointed out to Professor Barton their Eighth Ward materials. These included the remnants of Wert's original 35 newspaper articles pasted in a scrapbook many years ago by the diligent local historian Philip German, and a scrapbook of 60 Eighth Ward photographs compiled by Mrs. Clinton Leroy. Archivist Linda Ries of the Pennsylvania State Archives (PSA) in Harrisburg then advised Barton that additional Eighth Ward photographs were in their holdings, and archivist Michael Sherbon helped Barton identify 40 more in the files of the Bureau of Land Records. Finally, Ries found 76 more photographs in the J. Horace McFarland collection. Information on J. Howard Wert was graciously provided by Christine M. Amadure, reference archivist, and Karen Dupell, college archivist, at Gettysburg College; and also by Dr. Charles Gladfelter, executive director of the Adams County Historical Society, and Craig Caba, director of the Wert Gettysburg Collection. Funding for the transcription of Wert's articles was arranged by Professor William Mahar, former director of the School of Humanities at the Pennsylvania State University at Harrisburg, The Capital College. The transcription was executed by Linda Seaman. Jim Kempert of Arcadia Publishing was the skillful editor of the final manuscript.

PREFACE

The original newspaper articles were speckled with typographical errors. When it was obvious what Wert had intended to write, we corrected the mistake. If we could not decide whether a mistake had been made, we showed our puzzlement in brackets with a question mark. In a few cases where an entire line or at least several words appear to be missing from the text, we have not tried to guess what they were, but have simply indicated their absence.

The photographs of the Eighth Ward appear to have been taken both a few years before and a few years after Wert's articles were published. He was not the only documentarian of this disappearing neighborhood. Nearly all the photographs in both the HSDC and PSA collections have their locations identified, most often with the name of the intersection where the photographer stood. In the PSA collection, a few photos are identified as "May 3, 1917, J.D. Lemer." This refers to John Dunlap Lemer (1852–1931), younger brother of LeRue Lemer Sr. (1837–1920), who was one of Harrisburg's most active photographers. The Lemers' photography firm was the longest continuously operating business in the city's history. A few other photos in the PSA collection are marked "Please return to Harrisburg Park Commission, Harrisburg, PA." J. Horace McFarland took his 76 photos in 1904, 1909, and 1917.

All newspaper clippings are from the Harrisburg *Telegraph* from January through June, 1902.

In the introduction, the section on Wert's life was written by Professor Barton, who also researched and wrote the photo captions. The commentary on Wert's writing is the work of Professor Dorman.

INTRODUCTION

J. Howard Wert's "Passing of the Old Eighth" premiered on the editorial page of the Harrisburg *Patriot* on November 18, 1912. No banners, no pronouncements, heralded the debut. Tucked between light editorials and light prose, Wert's first article in the series of 35 to come simply materialized on the page—as if it, like the Old Eighth Ward itself, had always been a part of the landscape.

The *Patriot*'s editorial voice, *c.* 1912–1913, reflected the well-being of a relatively well-off metropolis. This was to be expected, for the newspaper was owned by the city's turn-of-the-century progressive mayor Vance C. McCormick, who along with his fellow reformers Mira Lloyd Dock and J. Horace McFarland had made the capital city a well-known specimen of the "City Beautiful" movement. Main streets were being paved for the first time, parks established, water systems modernized, and police and fire departments straightened out. Adjacent to the Old Eighth Ward, on top of a hill in the middle of the city, sat Pennsylvania's new capitol building, a structure President Theodore Roosevelt called the most excellent of its kind when he spoke at its dedication in 1906. Factories, locomotives, and citizens alike were humming.

Like all the local dailies, including its arch competitor the *Telegraph*, the *Patriot* positioned itself as a regional booster. The lead editorial that November 18 asked readers the following:

> Are we doing all that we can do and ought to do, to attract attention and push our own interests, or are we depending too much upon our splendid location, our unsurpassed railroad facilities and the reputation for enlightenment and progress that have been achieved during the last ten years?

New York City, the *Patriot* noted, had actually slipped in status over the past decade. Harrisburg could not afford to follow suit. Commercial decline posed a frightening specter. Any understrains of anxiety, however, dissolved into the editorial's major chords of probity, prosperity, and progress.

Wert's "Passing of the Old Eighth," awash in images of decrepitude and vice, would cast a shadow on the sunshine of the *Patriot*'s editorial page. Nominally the history of a ne'er-do-well neighborhood, the series was also a study of the effects of "progress." With the Old Eighth Ward soon to be razed for the Capitol Park extension, Wert asked *Patriot* readers to mull the cost of making the city beautiful.

The breadth of his intellect, coupled with his literary ambitions, lend the "Passing of the Old Eighth" its distinctive flavor. If Wert's multifaceted prose seems out of place in the *Patriot*, it appears less atypical when placed in the broader context of Progressive Era journalism. Newspaper and magazine writing at the turn of the twentieth century was, by and large, flashier—more narrative-based, less "objective"—than the journalism that superseded it by mid-century. Like his better-known peers Stephen Crane, Jacob Riis, Richard Harding Davis, Ida Tarbell, and Lincoln Steffens, Wert tapped a variety of literary traditions to woo, and sway, readers. His series of articles would interweave regionalism, muckraking, sentiment, and sensation.

Wert was no consistent craftsman. Long stretches of his saga lie flat on the page. Episodes are awkwardly spliced and oddly truncated. Such inconsistency, however, well-serves the literary sleuth. For when his writing does come alive we cannot help but notice. Wert writes dutifully of hearth, church, and school. He writes divinely of brothel, gambling den, and saloon. Each jump from workmanlike to inspired prose signals the awakened presence of an artist and social commentator.

J. Howard Wert (the J. stood for John, which he rarely used) was born on February 12, 1841, on a farm in Mt. Joy Township near Gettysburg, Pennsylvania. His father Adam Wert was a prominent abolitionist and his mother, the former Catherine Houghtelin, was a leader in Pennsylvania Methodism. As a child, he

This image of J. Howard Wert is from one of his own books, and shows the vigorous teacher and writer at the peak of his career. His articles on the Eighth Ward were written in his 70s.

attended country schools. As a young man, he studied at Gettysburg College, graduating with his B.A. in 1861. Wert then commenced his career as an educator. He taught in the Gettysburg schools from 1861 to 1864, was school principal there from 1866 to 1869, and then served as Adams County superintendent of schools until 1872. In 1874, he moved to Harrisburg to teach at Boys' High, becoming principal of that school in 1879. After 14 years in that post, he was appointed in 1893 the first principal of Harrisburg High School, also known as Central. Altogether, he was a school man for 33 years.

His wife Emma Letitia Aughinbaugh, whom he married in 1869, was also a teacher and native of Gettysburg. They were the parents of four sons and a daughter: Howard, who became a postal clerk in Harrisburg; Edward, Gettysburg College class of 1895 and a capital city attorney; Samuel, superintendent of the Harrisburg Pipe and Pipe Bending Works; Frank, a newspaperman and public relations manager; and Annie, supervisor of primary schools in Harrisburg. They were loyal Lutherans, attending Harrisburg's Zion church at Fourth and Market Streets.

Wert was a deeply devoted student of the Civil War, and was often said to have collected every significant publication on the Gettysburg battle. He was a charter member of the Grand Army of the Republic in the state. His writings about the war include *A Complete Hand-book of the Monuments . . . on the Gettysburg Battlefield* (1886); *The Two Great Armies at Gettysburg* (1890); *History of the 209th Regiment, Pennsylvania Volunteer Infantry* (1894); and *Historical Souvenir of the Fiftieth Anniversary of the Battle of Gettysburg, July 1-4, 1913* (1913). He was also the author of a collection of verse, *Poems of Camp and Hearth*, his most cited publication, which he began writing in 1859 and had published in 1887.

Wert became a student of the Civil War after he lived through and fought in it. He wrote in his battlefield *Hand-Book* that "during the three fierce days of conflict of July, 1863," he "saw for miles along right and left and centre, rows of heaped and mangled dead." In the succeeding months "he daily wandered" over the battlefield, and "during each succeeding summer" he "strolled again and again over familiar scenes," determining that he should write "a work which shall render this field a durable study to both soldier and civilian for all the ages of the future." His experience as a civilian eyewitness to the Gettysburg battle, a collector of its relics, and, reportedly, a scout for Union generals, would become the basis for his many writings and his expertise on the subject.

A year after the Gettysburg battle, Wert enlisted in the 209th Pennsylvania Volunteer Infantry Regiment, which was organized at Camp Curtin in Harrisburg. He was mustered in to Company G with other troops from Adams County in September, 1864, was promoted from sergeant to first sergeant on January 2, 1865, then promoted to second lieutenant on February 13, 1865. According to Samuel Bates's *History of Pennsylvania Volunteers* (1871), this regiment saw limited action, mainly fatigue duty at fortifications and road building near the James River in Virginia. On March 25, 1865, however, they were successful in repulsing a Confederate attack near Fort Steadman, where 5 members of the regiment were killed, 50 wounded, and 350 enemy prisoners taken. Then, on April 2, they were engaged in battle near Fort Sedgwick outside Petersburg, Virginia, with 7 killed and 52 wounded, but capturing the enemy ground and many prisoners. The regiment was afterwards in charge of army trains until the end of the war, being mustered out on May 31, 1865.

Some of the details of Wert's post-bellum life as an educator can be found coincidentally in his book *Annals of the Boys' High School of Harrisburg, 1875-1893*, which he wrote for the school in 1895. He tells that, in his early years, he supervised from 40 to 60 pupils in a single room, either teaching them himself or sending them to other teachers' recitation rooms. In his later years, Wert taught, at various times throughout the week, Latin, Greek, Roman history, English history, physical geography, natural history, physiology, government, philosophy, reading, rhetoric, composition, spelling, and declamation. When he became principal, his teaching load was reduced by half to only seven courses per week. His salary ranged from $67.50 to $110 per month during his tenure. Classes ran from 9:00 a.m. to 5:00 p.m., breaking for lunch from noon until 2:00 p.m. School was in session about 180 days per year and enrollment topped off at around 80 boys—in a city of about 40,000 persons.

On one occasion, after completing their formal, public examinations, his Latin pupils presented him with a fancy gold pen, holder, and inkstand. Another time, before they left on vacation, students gave him a great turkey. Seniors once awarded him a box of choice cigars, but "unfortunately, he had stopped smoking," the principal noted. Perhaps his pupils were saluting him for his performance skills as well as his position—it was said Wert could quote 60,000 lines of English and American poetry. Or maybe this phenomenon was what the school board had in mind when it praised him for possessing "superior disciplinary and systematic qualities."

Wert's Boys' High featured solemn ceremonies having "tasty mechanical execution," as he put it in the *Annals*. At graduation exercises held at the Grand Opera House, seniors orated on subjects such as "The Anglo-Saxon Race," "America for Americans," and "Every Man the Architect of His Own Fortune." (At Girls' High School, the topics included "Umbrellas," "Faces," and "Is this World a Vale of Tears?") The school had a proper Christmas reception every year, and it celebrated Arbor Day with speeches on particular trees. For these occasions, music was regularly provided by the Metronome Orchestra.

We can tell from the history he wrote and from his own testimony that Wert was a progressive thinker on race relations. As a school principal, he called for fair treatment of minority students. In the *Annals*, he wrote proudly about three black pupils who were admitted in 1879. When the boys graduated in 1883, two of them with honors, Wert noted:

> The problem that had caused some so much trepidation had been solved. Well does the author recall the terrible prognostications made by well-meaning people in regard to a ruined school system and impending

This Fender 1881 bird's-eye view of Harrisburg shows the most notorious section of the Eighth Ward from the capitol grounds to the Pennsylvania Railroad and Pennsylvania Canal.

bloodshed if these boys were admitted to the same school with scions of the Caucasian race. It required a firm administration of government to secure exact justice at first. The author is proud of the fact that if he won no other laurel in his nineteen years of service in the Harrisburg High School, it has been universally conceded . . . on every occasion all were treated with impartial justice without regard to religious belief, financial standing, race, or color.

To underscore this claim, Wert quoted from a letter later sent to him by the Reverend William H. Marshall, one of those three students:

I remember public sentiment did not altogether favor our admission, and but for your determination to see that poor and rich, white and black, influential and non-influential, were equal before the law, our years might, nay, would have been much less pleasant.

William Howard Day, president of the Harrisburg School Board from 1891 to 1893 and the city's most distinguished black leader, testified in the *Annals'* preface as to Wert's notable fairness:

One of the main elements of his success, and one of the reasons for pupil and parent and school director reposing confidence in him, was the practical exemplification in this relationship of the motto of his whole life, namely, "To exercise exact justice to all without regard to wealth, race, or religion." In his domain, all had equal chance. All were treated fairly.

It should be noted that the Harrisburg school district had been racially segregated since its founding in 1869, so such fair treatment would have been especially noticeable.

At the end of the *Annals*, Wert announced that he "withdrew" from school work in Harrisburg because, at age 53, he was unsatisfied with its compensations. He named a dozen schools the same size as Harrisburg High School that typically paid their principals about twice as much as his $1,100 yearly salary. He then listed 19 schools that were smaller than his but still paid principals about twice as much. Trying for diplomacy, he concluded the following:

> Whilst from a personal standpoint, I might perhaps wish now that, during the past nineteen years, the same education and labor had been given to some other vocation, I can never regret the thousands of warm friendships formed with graduates, pupils, parents, and school officials.

After resigning in 1894, Wert "engaged in literary work" for the remainder of his career, according to his college's alumni records. He contributed articles and poems to more than 100 publications (another source says 400) and penned schoolbooks such as *School Composition Work Made Attractive*. Among his other book titles are *The Mystic League of Three* (the first novel he wrote when a sophomore at Gettysburg College), *God's Centennial*, *Rhyme and Reason*, *Alecto and Ebony*, and *Five Years in the Grave*. The "Passing of the Old Eighth" was one of his last publications.

His final years were spent residing in a pleasant row house near the intersection of North Second and Forster Streets, only a few blocks from the Old Eighth. He was 80 when he died, after a long illness, on the evening of March 11, 1920. "He had hundreds of staunch friends in Harrisburg who will miss his friendly interest and cheerful greeting," reported a local newspaper. His obituary in the *Gettysburg Compiler* headlined that the "Professor" had "Never Tired Singing the Praises of the Old Home Place." A few days later, the morning train brought Wert's body back to Gettysburg, where it was met by his sons and his Civil War comrades, who escorted it to the grave in Evergreen Cemetery.

Wert's prose reflects two early twentieth century impulses: one toward generalization, the other toward particularization. While reform of the period developed an increasingly national focus, popular fiction, especially magazine fiction, continued to feature the "local color" style that had emerged after the Civil War. Wert's history of the Old Eighth looks outward and inward both: a detailed study of a single urban ward, it asks far-reaching questions about America's transition from the nineteenth century into the twentieth.

New print technologies, new circulation strategies, and a new emphasis on reform transformed the role, and the reach, of Progressive Era mass media.

Popular magazines like *McClure's*, *Everybody's*, *Cosmopolitan*, and even *The Ladies' Home Journal* began to showcase investigative reporting. Muckraking exposés like Lincoln Steffens's "The Shame of the Cities" and Upton Sinclair's *The Jungle* made local concerns (voter fraud in Philadelphia, tainted meat in Chicago) into national concerns. The historian Richard Hofstadter argued persuasively in *The Age of Reform* that the novelty of muckraking "was neither its ideas nor its existence, but its reach—its nationwide character and its capacity to draw nationwide attention, the presence of mass muckraking media with national circulation, and huge resources for the research that went into exposure." A nation of readers, divided by region and class, was unified by pique.

At the same time that muckraking journals awakened the nation to a sense of shared outrage, others recalled readers to their roots. Publications like *The Atlantic Monthly*, *Harper's Monthly*, and *The Century*—self-appointed guardians of American literary culture—declined to ride the muckraking bandwagon. Fiction, not nonfiction, would remain their forte, and regional fiction would remain their particular pride. Sarah Orne Jewett, Hamlin Garland, Helen Hunt Jackson, Bret Harte, and other regional writers had dominated the pages of the "genteel" journals in the late nineteenth century. Their successors continued to sound the nostalgic note in the new century. By documenting local folkways, these writers helped preserve a way of life that was passing.

This view from the far east end of South Street looks westward back through the Eighth Ward to the state capitol building. The corner house on the right advertises a room for rent as well as dress making, Cinco cigars, and Honest Scrap. (HSDC)

15

J. Howard Wert was on the record as a proponent of the Harrisburg park extension. He had editorialized, on February 1, 1906, about the need for additional grounds "to set off to best advantage the superb building just completed." Now, with a number of downtown landmarks ("some famous, some infamous") slated for destruction, Wert set out to write "the history of 'the Old Eighth' about to lapse into oblivion."

Wert's "history" would take the form of an urban pastoral: a saga of paradise regained, at uncertain cost. On the surface, the Eighth seemed ripe for a makeover. Here sat some of the city's roughest and most crime-ridden terrain. "If the Old Eighth Ward should become a thing of beauty now," Wert mused, "it will be more than much of it has been in the past." Perhaps so, perhaps not. Again and again, throughout the series, Wert returns to the theme of beauty—and suggests that stock formulations fail him. Can beauty be found in an alley? Can it be lost in a garden? And how is a historian to gauge the aesthetics of progress?

Consider the wording of Wert's mission statement of November 25, 1912: "The articles of this series will be devoted exclusively to buildings, individuals and events of the older portion of the Eighth Ward which is about to pass from the map except as a restful breathing spot and a garden of beauty." And again, on

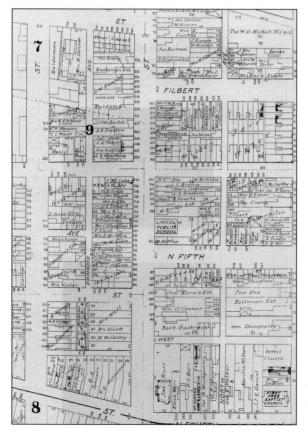

The 1889 Roe Atlas of the City of Harrisburg includes this detailed map of the Eighth Ward. This section shows the northern half of the ward from Briggs Street on the left to State Street on the right. (North is to the left.)

March 24 of the following year: "It is the intention of the writer to give some account, in this series of every prominent industry which has flourished in the Eighth Ward ere it disappears to be replaced by a beautiful park." The words "beauty" and "beautiful" seem almost like afterthoughts. The "buildings, individuals and events" of the Old Eighth, the "flourishing" industry: these images, not the "beautiful park," take precedence and, in Wert's telling, acquire a strange beauty of their own.

Wert is neither so enamored of the underworld, nor so blinded by nostalgia, that he overlooks urban malaise. Instead he strikes a balance, celebrating the vibrancy of the Old Eighth while acknowledging and contextualizing the neighborhood's failings. At no point does he appear more quintessentially "progressive" than when he bemoans the lack of green space. Sounding much like Jacob Riis, he notes that downtown Harrisburg bears witness to the "utilitarian ideas of getting as many buildings as possible on as little ground as possible and, consequently, reaping as large returns in rents as possible." Furthermore, like so many Progressive Era reformers, Wert links material deprivations to spiritual dissolution. After describing one notorious bawdy hall he rages:

> Any social or governmental condition that permits the existence of the life of which the 'Red Lion' was typical, is rotten and defective somewhere. Civic betterment means more fine buildings, clean streets, parks and playgrounds. It means also civic purity.

For a twenty-first century reader, the apparent schizophrenic quality of Wert's prose can be off-putting. Pious at one moment, hard-nosed at another, folksy at the next turn, the "Passing of the Old Eighth" veers wildly among literary modes and moods. Considered, however, from an early twentieth century perspective, Wert's piebald style seems less self-conflicted. The melding of a nineteenth-century moral sensibility and a "modern" appreciation for "progress" made Wert's work accessible to his contemporaries.

Thus in chapter 12, Wert turns his attention to the Garfield school for little girls. His language is evocative, sentimental:

> It is a sight to melt the heart of a stoic to see the wee tots gather in front of the school room door of a pleasant morning watching for the appearance of the teacher. Many a matron will read this sketch to whom will be recalled the happy school days of a fourth or third of a century ago when they were of the bevy of happy hearts that met daily for delightful school work in the old frame shop.

Wert ends the vignette by observing that the school site, on Fourth Street, "has now been purchased by the State and has disappeared from history forever." The abrupt transition from presence to absence begs the question: whither the values of "a fourth or third of a century ago"? Have they, too, "disappeared" in the course

This section of the 1889 Roe map shows the southern half of the ward from State Street on the left to Walnut Street on the right. The names on the properties are the owners of record, not necessarily those who lived there.

of urban renewal? The sentimental language here helps foster a perspective wary of progress.

Or does it? Each installment of Wert's saga must be read as an episode in a serial narrative—and the chapter on the Garfield school directly follows a chapter on the "colored" schools of Harrisburg. Here, then, is how Wert makes the transition from one chapter to the next:

> While the colored children of the Eighth Ward were packed, like sardines
> in a box, in the uncomfortable and unsanitary rooms of the 'Jennings'
> school . . . the Harrisburg School board found it incumbent upon them
> to make some provision for the little white girls of the district.

Subsequent references to "happy hearts" and "wee tots" no longer ring quite as clear. And progress—change—no longer connotes loss: if the Old Eighth featured racial inequity, all hail the new.

As the critic Benedict Anderson reminds us in *Imagined Communities*, newspapers create community. Wert's *Patriot* articles perform the work of community-building in the face of community-razing. Wert writes the following in an early chapter:

> The removal of many buildings from the Second Street and Meadow
> Lane section, including the old St. Nicholas church and the old hotel
> which was the first home of the 'Washy' Hose Company, is within the
> memory of the youngest reader.

In the same installment, he refers to "the famed 'Steamboat' hotel and other well known structures of the past." The personal tone reminds readers—even the youngest—of their membership, and stake, in the community.

Wert practically revels in description of vice: "There were orgies by day, and fiercer orgies by night that were protracted till the stars had paled before the brightening eastern skies." Recognizing that readers might misconstrue his motives, Wert follows dish with disclaimer:

> To prevent any possible misapprehension, I wish to say again, most
> emphatically, that, although disgraceful vice conditions were in
> evidence, year after year, in the "Old Eighth," yet has it always been the
> home of many devoted and noble men and women whose unsullied
> lives shine all the more brightly by the contrast.

Still, scoundrels bring out the best in Wert.

David Reynolds discusses the allure of the so-called "sympathetic criminal" in his classic study *Beneath the American Renaissance*. From Hester Prynne to Ahab to the assorted antiheroes of antebellum crime sheets, "bad" characters were embraced as fervently—by writers and readers both—as their "good" counterparts. Wert, having adopted the sentimental tone of mid-nineteenth-century literature, also adopts the sympathetic criminal. He dwells on the exploits of cheats, fools, and boozers. In Harry Cook, "Billy Jelly," and other Eighth Ward heels, he creates his most memorable characters. What are we to make of the "sympathy" he so obviously feels for these ruffians?

Wert may simply be following sentimental tradition, introducing flawed individuals whose inevitable downfall serves as moral text. Perhaps, though, his aim is more subversive. By lavishing so much column space on Harrisburg's sinners, Wert forces readers to readjust their spheres of reference. Harry Cook stands at the convergence point of realism and romance, ready to insinuate himself into the comfort zone of Wert's readers.

Whatever the interpretation, we think Wert's history of the Old Eighth will find its way into our modern comfort zone, and even if we are inclined to smile at his style, we can still appreciate his description of the rambunctious, multi-racial, multi-ethnic city life that used to be. In the historiography of Harrisburg, there is no document to match this one for its detailed stories of the successes and scandals of this city's "Good Old Days."

Michael Barton and Jessica Dorman
Penn State University at Harrisburg

1. Early History of the
Old Eighth Ward

November 18, 1912

In an article published in a Harrisburg newspaper, February 1, 1906, I wrote as follows: "All the area from North street to Walnut and down to the line of 'the Pennsylvania's' trackage is needed for a park addition, to set off to best advantage the superb building just completed. That this will come is almost as certain as any future event can be. It is a matter that concerns not Harrisburg only, but the whole of our great Commonwealth. If the decree for park extension goes forth, you and I will wander over the grounds some pleasant day ere the demolition is completed, and chat together about some of the landmarks—some famous, some infamous—that made the present Eighth Ward a spot of note in Civil war days."

Well, the decree has gone forth and operations to make it effective are being carried on so actively, that it is high time for him to be busy who would write the history of "the Old Eighth" about to lapse into oblivion. In this series the writer proposes to give a bird's eye view of "the Eighth" of the present and the past, drawn from his own personal knowledge and from a mass of data obtained from many individuals and documentary sources.

Size of the Park Extension

The amount of ground to be taken over by the State for the extension of the Capitol Park is 29 acres, inclusive of the street areas, which are of considerable extent. The present Capitol Park is somewhat more than 15 acres, composed of four acres and twenty-one perches donated to the State by John Harris, the founder; ten acres purchased from William Maclay; and an aggregate of considerably more than an acre representing minor additions to round out the grounds, the most important of these being the High street triangle of which an account will be given in one of the opening numbers of this series.

The State, therefore, will have a total park area, inclusive of the ground on which the buildings stand, of approximately 45 acres. A goodly piece of land! And

An aerial photograph of the great crowd attending an appearance by President Franklin Roosevelt in 1936 shows all the work done. Rows of trees grow behind the Capitol Complex in the very orderly park, and next to the North Office Building nearly as much space has been given to a parking lot. (Pennsylvania State Archives [PSA])

yet the whole of it would be a mere truck patch in the eyes of a farmer of the pioneer days, for one of the earliest recollections of my youth is of a field on my father's farm known as the "eighty-acre field." But that field would have been well sold, in those days, at thirty dollars an acre. Here, in a small space, is a land value running into millions, whilst the events that have occurred upon the 29 acres under immediate consideration, would fill volumes. The aim of this series is to rescue some of them from obscurity.

A PARK EXTENSION THAT FAILED

Our Capitol Park would be yet larger had the plans of early legislators been carried out. To Harrisburgers a century ago, the space from South street to North between Second and Third was known as Maclay's swamp. It was always deep with water and mire, and was a famous skating place in the winter season. After rains the surplus water drained off sluggishly into the creek which, crossing Front street just above Walnut, emptied into the Susquehanna.

April 11, 1825, a resolution passed the Legislature providing for the purchase by the State of all the land between South street and North street from the line of Third street to Sweet Briar alley. It was ascertained that the amounts demanded by the several owners aggregated $24,400, whereupon the plan of adding this tract to the park was abandoned, the legislators deeming the price an exorbitant one.

In recent years the scheme for a park extension riverward was revived by ex-Governor Pennypacker, but received little attention because it was believed the present property values would be too great to be within the means of the Commonwealth.

ORIGIN OF THE EIGHTH WARD

Although the present park extension does not include nearly all of the Eighth Ward, it does include substantially all that was built up until within comparatively recent years. It wipes out the Eighth Ward of canal boating and Civil war days—the "Eighth Ward" of an almost Statewide celebrity.

No part of the Eighth Ward was included in the founders' original plot of the town. Various enlargements were made between 1785 and 1898, yet, at the end of this time, all of the present "Eighth" within the borough limits was the triangle included between Walnut and South streets and the line of the Fourth street of today, which street had not then been laid out north of Walnut street. This is shown by a map, bearing the date of 1791, now hanging in the Common Council chamber on the second floor of the Dauphin County Court House.

The remainder of the Eighth Ward west of Paxton Creek did not come within the borough limits until 1838, when Herr street was made the municipality's northern boundary between the Susquehanna and the creek. The Allison Hill portion of the Eighth is a yet much later addition.

At one time the borough of Harrisburg was divided into North and South Wards; but, some time before it became a city, it was divided into four wards for voting purposes. For school purposes the original division into North and South Wards was retained until the revised charter of 1868 created the consolidated Harrisburg district.

When the city of Harrisburg was created in 1869, it was divided into six wards, the two additional wards, the Fifth and Sixth, being but sparsely populated at that time.

The Eighth Ward of the city of Harrisburg was created by an act of the Legislature approved April 22, 1868, it being composed of that portion of the old Fourth Ward which was east of the Capitol Park.

An act passed by the Legislature in accordance with a provision of the Constitution of 1873, enabled that Court to divide the Eighth Ward into two precincts. The other wards divided into two precincts, at this early period, were the First and Sixth.

2. STREET PLOTTING AND MODES OF BUILDING

NOVEMBER 25, 1912

The increase of population in the Eighth Ward and especially the building up in recent years of large areas on Allison's Hill which were but farm lands when the ward was created, have necessitated the increase of the number of precincts from two to five. As new precincts were formed there was some recasting, from time to time, of the original lines.

As the lines now run the First, Second and Fourth precincts extend from the line of Fourth street to the railroad. The First is between Walnut street and South alley and when South alley ends at the market house, the line deflects to South street. The Second extends from the northern boundary of the First to North alley. The Fourth is comprised between North alley and Forster street.

It will be seen, therefore, that the Capitol Park Extension, in taking all the territory from Fourth street to the P.R.R. [Pennsylvania Railroad] between the lines of Walnut and North streets, covers all of the First and Second and a portion of the Fourth precincts of the Ward. The Third and Fifth precincts, being entirely east of the railroad are, of course, untouched.

The articles of this series will be devoted exclusively to buildings, individuals and events of the older portion of the Eighth Ward which is about to pass from the map except as a restful breathing spot and a garden of beauty.

LABYRINTH OF STREETS AND COURTS

And, if the Old Eighth Ward should become a thing of beauty now, it will be more than much of it has been in the past. With the exception of State street, the width of which was dictated by its relation to the Capitol, the streets are generally narrow, whilst some of them are crooked and others go wandering off at all sorts of angles with no uniformity of plotting. In fact, some of them do not appear to have been laid out by an official authority, but rather to have leaped into existence on the good old plan of some one starting to build along a cow path or a lane. One can see here, on a small scale, all the irregularities and intricacies which made the "Old Town" of Baltimore before the big fire, lower New York, and the heart of old Boston such marvels of perplexity. Here are little blind courts, too narrow for any vehicle to use, into which little of God's free air or sunlight can enter, closely built up and every tenement teeming with life.

ARCHITECTURAL CONDITIONS

In the earlier days of Harrisburg building some queer things were done. With large expanses of open territory all around, it seemed to have become the fixed idea of owners and contractors that every inch of ground must be occupied. Not a foot of ground must be wasted at the front, at the side, in the rear, anywhere, in the foolishness of having a lawn, a flower bed or a yard of any kind.

The notions as to the sacred preciousness of every inch of ground and the impiety of using any of it for any purpose but building on, ran riot, half a century ago, in every part of Harrisburg; but in no locality was it carried out so completely as in the old portion of the Eighth Ward. Go look at the very labyrinth of nondescript frames still in existence in many parts of the space between Walnut and North streets. You can then see how completely all ideas of beauty, or even ordinary comeliness of architecture; all attempts at even elementary comfort or sanitation have been slaughtered before utilitarian ideas of getting as many buildings as possible on as little ground as possible and, consequently, reaping as large returns in rents as possible.

As the streets, alleys and courts of this section were generally narrow and close together the houses erected on the front of a lot ran back till they met those that were built to face the rearward alley. Go to any rear balcony or window, and you have beneath you a very maze of back buildings and sheds.

Thus the houses of Walnut street are cheek by jowl with those of Tanner, Short and Christie's court; those of South alley with those of South street on the one side and State street on the other; and so on through all the sandwich-like juxtaposition of houses.

The thoroughfares taken entirely by the Capitol Park Extension are East Cranberry, Tanner, Short, Filbert, Poplar, East South and the former Spruce streets, South, North market house and Angle alleys, and Christie's court. The street formerly called Spruce is now known officially as North Fifth, for North Fifth is spread over the city in disjointed sections. The highways taken in part are Cowden, North Fourth, State and West streets, with North and Walnut as boundary streets as with the present park.

3. A Former Capitol Park Extension

December 2, 1912

Before plunging into a minute description of the leading matters of interest on the site of the present Capitol Park extension, I wish to tell of a former extension which involved the razing of buildings, an account of which will be new, in all probability, to many of the present generation.

Although Harrisburg is but little more than a century and a quarter of age, the demolition of old dwelling houses and the abandonment of their site as a residential section has been going on for many years on a large scale. Down among the iron works of South Harrisburg, whole rows of cottages have disappeared as the growing mills demanded more room.

But railroad expansion has been the greatest factor. Along the line of the P.R.R., from the lower end of the city to far above State street, buildings have disappeared in quantities as greater trackage was demanded. Where Paxton and Indian streets adjoin the railroad a large number of houses have gone down in recent years. The removal of many buildings from the Second street and Meadow Lane section, including the old St. Nicholas church and the old hotel which was the first home of the "Washy" Hose Company, is within the memory of the youngest reader.

In the vicinity of the Pennsylvania passenger station the work has been extensive. Not only the quaint old station of the P.R.R. and N.C. railroads, but all that row of buildings facing it, have gone. Amongst these were the Temperance Hotel, conducted by Theodore Boyer, father of the present efficient poor director and juvenile joy giver, Charles L. Boyer, as well as a series of hotels and restaurants with high sounding names, as Empire House and the like.

From Market street have gone the famed "Steamboat" hotel and other well known structures of the past. From Market to State streets the changes have been radical. Amongst the buildings that have disappeared are the Baumgardner House, also called the State's Union at one time, the Iron City hotel and the collection of saloons and liquor stores that, facing Canal Street, once clustered just below the State street bridge, as well as the old Zingari Bitters building that towered amongst the tracks till recently.

THE GROWTH OF CAPITOL PARK

Capitol Park as it now stands has been a gradual growth. To the four acres and twenty-one perches donated by John Harris, the founder, the State added ten acres purchased from William Maclay. But to carry out his contract with the State, Maclay was obliged to purchase from the owners a number of the Harris lots which lay between Harris' donation and his own land. For the Harris gift to the State extended only to the line of Pine street, whilst the borough's northern boundary was South street, where it adjoined the Maclay tract, known in early Harrisburg history as Maclaysburg. Some other slight additions were made, at various times, to round out the plot.

HIGH STREET THROUGH CAPITOL GROUNDS

But there was one blemish on the Capitol Park symmetry that, in time, became a decided eyesore both to the State officials and the citizens. The map of 1791, on the walls of the Council Chamber in the Court House, shows Fourth street ending at Walnut, whilst from a point about opposite to the old John Donner

This photograph of State Street, looking east from a capitol balcony, was taken between 1904 and 1909, and shows the Eighth Ward still dense with buildings and fairly busy. Compare with the 1917 photograph from the same perspective on p. 47. (PSA)

hotel, a street, named High, ran northward. The map of 1843, in the same room, shows Fourth street extended northward to Cranberry at which point it was intersected by High street which then continued northward on about the present line of Fourth. The point of intersection was about where an angle can be seen today in Fourth street and in the Capitol Park embankment. High street passed just east of the old Arsenal buildings which were located in the lower part of the Capitol grounds.

The triangle formed by Walnut, High and Fourth street was thickly built up. On Fourth, near the Junction with High, stood the Frisch brewery running back to High street. North of the brewery were two dwelling houses, one of which is remembered by the older citizens as a nondescript roughcast house facing on High street with three stories, but having four stories on the Fourth street side on account of a basement entrance.

South of the brewery there was a frame building on Fourth Street, whilst at the corner of Fourth and Walnut was a hotel kept by a Jewish Rabbi named Barnhart and subsequently by a Mr. Kelly. Of the buildings along the Walnut street side of the triangle, one was occupied for many years by a Mr. Rupp, a celebrated old time pretzel baker. At Walnut and High streets was the coach building shop of Joseph Sayford, who resided on Fourth below Walnut in the house now occupied by his son-in-law, Charles E. Metzger.

With the construction of pike roads, which enabled vehicles to replace horseback travel, the building of carriages became a great industry in Pennsylvania. In this State were made most of the pleasure conveyances which were disposed of in southern markets. Sayford conducted one of the several coach shops in Harrisburg which, about the middle of the last century, did excellent work and gave employment to a considerable number of merchants.

It required persistent missionary work and years of agitation to secure for the State, as an addition to Capitol Park, the properties located on the triangle just described. This was finally brought to a culmination in 1873. The purchase was passed by the Harrisburg Council April 12, of that year. The records of the Auditor General's department at the Capitol show that the purchases were made in July, 1873. George F. Ross, of the Department of Internal Affairs, at that time a clerk in the office of Attorney General Samuel E. Dimmick and Deputy Attorney General Lyman D. Gilbert, on the last day of 1873, served notices on the occupants of the several properties to vacate on or before April 1, 1874. The work of demolition took place as soon as the properties were vacated.

I find in the vaults of the Secretary of Internal Affairs the following record of the prices paid: beginning with the apex of the triangle at the junction of Fourth and High street, Gilnaugh, $2,000; Hummel (half interest), $1,250; Frisch (a half interest), $1,250; Frisch brewery, $21,000; the Rupp heirs, $3,900. All of the above properties fronted on Fourth street. Hotel at Fourth and Walnut, adjacent property on Walnut street, Mrs. Theodore Adams, $9,200; Rupp (bakery), $3,900; Sayford (coach shop), $7,200. Total purchase price of properties in the extension, $49,700. The Mr. Gilnaugh owning the first property mentioned was the father of "Chiefy" Gilnaugh. It will thus be seen that "the Chiefy" comes honestly by his interest in the Capitol grounds and buildings, for it was on this very spot he spent his juvenile days.

From a very valuable map of Harrisburg, dated 1850, in the office of the Secretary of Internal Affairs, I learn that in that year the Gilnaugh house was owned by M. Bourk (also spelled Burke at another place) whilst the only other building then facing on Fourth street was the property of Mr. Simon. J. Morsch owned the corner hotel building and the remaining lots on Walnut street belonged to J.F. Williams, K. Rupp and Mr. Simon.

The old Arsenal standing west of High street, no doubt, had been handsome in the days of its youth. But, in 1874, it had a gone-to-seed appearance that made it as grotesquely antique as an old maid in a sunbonnet in the midst of a group of cheery school girls. So it, too, ceased to exist, and late in the fall of 1874 men were busily engaged in leveling and grading what is now the southeast section of Capitol Park. All the stately and umbrageous trees of that part of the park have been the product of thirty-seven years. There was not a tree there till the spring of 1875.

South Street ran east–west inside the Eighth Ward. This view looks east down South Street from the capitol at Fourth Street to the end of the neighborhood. (PSA)

4. Politics and Politicians

December 9, 1912

The Eighth Ward citizens always took their politics very seriously. But when, in the early seventies of the last century, under the fifteenth amendment to the federal constitution, the right of suffrage again came to the crowded colored population of positions of the Ward, the scenes around the various polling places were lurid. There had been a time when the colored man in Pennsylvania voted. He had been deprived of that privilege when the constitution of 1838 inserted the word "white" in the qualifications of elections. It was on account of that one invidious word that the Great Commoner, Thaddeus Stevens, a member of the convention, refused to sign the instrument which it produced.

There were a number of colored men in Harrisburg, who had voted prior to 1838, who, in the seventies, after a lapse of more than thirty years, were again enabled to exercise the elective franchise. Those who were opposed to the extension of the franchise to the colored race tried to prevent them from voting by challenges and other means. Then things became troublesome and vociferous around the polling places.

The colored voters soon found able champions in their own ranks. One of my abiding recollections is of burly Major John W. Simpson mounted on a store box near the polling window at Umberger's Cross Keys hotel, which stood on the eastern side of Filbert street, at the corner of Walnut. As the perspiring Major shouted and gesticulated, he generally bore down all opposition and put through all the multitudinous voters he brought to the polls and for whom he vouched.

An Unequal Contest

In the days when the Eighth Ward had but two precincts, the first was spoken of as the negro, the second as an Irish bailiwick. At first it seemed to be nip and tuck between the two precincts for supremacy in the control of the Ward. But the Irish did not increase in numbers. In fact many of them were removing to other sections. On the other hand the colored vote appeared to be a constantly augmenting factor.

A few days ago a prominent city official and I were looking at a recently taken photograph of Christie's Court, a little blind alley with a narrow entrance but no exit, running from Cranberry street in the direction of Walnut, and closely packed with some half dozen houses.

"My," said the official, "didn't there used to be a registration in there?"

"And they all voted the Republican ticket?" said I.

"Of course," was the reply.

Those were the days when the attempt to form a Democratic colored club would have been a bid for a mob, almost for a lynching.

VOTING PLACES IN PARK EXTENSION

The shifting of precinct lines and other causes have combined to make a considerable number of locations within the bounds of the present park extension polling places during the past forty years.

Once it was regarded in Harrisburg as a religious duty to use every school building in the city as a voting place. To this arrangement every kid in the public schools gave enthusiastic and patriotic assent, for all the schools were closed on election day; and, all rooms in which elections were held, the day following,

This photograph shows the west side of Filbert Street, looking north from Walnut Street to South Street and beyond. (HSDC)

The Frisby Battis corner, favored by African-American Harrisburgers, is across Fifth Street (also called Spruce Street) from Parson's Drug Store. (HSDC)

whilst janitors removed the tobacco quids, cigar butts, whiskey flasks and other paraphernalia necessary to the exercise of the right of suffrage.

Thus it came that the Day School building on North street and the little one-story, one-room shop on Fourth street, near the Mt. Vernon Hook and Ladder Company, known as the Garfield School, were both, for many years, polling places. Other voting locations have been the Cross Keys Hotel, Filbert and Walnut streets; the Citizens' engine house; the Frisby Battis corner, Short and South streets; the Mt. Vernon fire house, and the annex to the State street market. Around all these have been tempestuous times as hotly contested elections were fought to a finish.

COLORED POLITICAL LEADERS

But, as in many other places, the colored brother, in the "Old Eighth" Ward, learned the political game promptly and thoroughly. He took kindly to practical politics and often beat his teacher. Some of the earlier colored political leaders in the Ward were William Battis, who died a few years ago in Middletown, and Major John W. Simpson, both of whom were elected to the alderman's office in the Ward; Constable William Harley, Ward Assessor George Galbraith, who died very recently, Frisby Battis, and Rev. Prof. William Howard Day, for many years an efficient member of the Harrisburg school board and at one time its president.

The deals political that were made, the tricks political that were pulled off in the Old Eighth Ward, during the past forty years would fill, not a newspaper article, but a volume of unabridged dictionary size. I am not recounting any of them for I am not hunting trouble.

Some of the men who went into "the Ward" the night before the election, with a good fat roll, have passed over the silent river. But there are those who will, as they read this article, smile quietly and knowingly at the recollection of things that have been done.

Persons of both parties, who were political factors in the Ward, will be alluded to, from time to time, in our trips through the business and residential sections of the new park extension.

St. Lawrence Catholic Church on Walnut Street was also known as St. Lawrence German Catholic Church. (HSDC)

5. Churches in the Park Extension

December 16, 1912

Persons whose business it has been to make the enumeration, tell me there are 527 business and residential buildings in the Capitol Park extension district. I visited every one of them annually, for many years, but never counted them, and am quite satisfied now to take the toll of the authorities.

Of the above number five are prominent churches, viz: St. Lawrence Roman Catholic church on Walnut street near Fifth; the Wesley Union A.M.E. Zion on South street, corner of Tanner; the Bethel A.M.E. Zion church on State street, corner of West; the Kesher Israel synagogue on State street, corner of Fourth; and the Chisuk Emuna synagogue on Filbert street, corner of North alley.

Of these the most extensive in the amount of ground covered by the church edifice and its supplementary buildings is:

The St. Lawrence Catholic Church

And it is of it I propose to speak in this number. In doing this I have supplemented the facts already in my possession with additional information obtained recently in a very pleasant interview with the present rector of the church, the courteous Father Peter S. Huegel.

The St. Lawrence congregation was organized by Father Dryer, of York, April, 1859. After his death Father Meurer took charge. From January 1, 1860, the congregation was visited and services held regularly twice a month, the Rev. M.J. Meurer and the Rev. J. Vollmeyer attending.

At first the new organization worshiped in a rented hall, but in November, 1860, it purchased an old church building on Front street, between Walnut and Locust. Several different rectors officiated up to January, 1869, when that grand man, Father Clemens A. Koppernagle was placed in charge. He immediately began planning to give the congregation a new and permanent home commensurate with the size of the membership built up under his efficient ministrations.

In the Fall of 1873 the Front street church was sold to Henry Gilbert and the following Spring the purchase of the Walnut street site was consummated. This was admirably selected and admirably located for the needs of the growing church. It was an L-shaped piece of ground with a frontage on Walnut street on which the church building faced, whilst the shorter arm of the L ran out to Short street fronting on it from Angle alley to a point more than half way down to Walnut street. On this front are erected the parochial school building, the home of the rector and the house devoted to the Sisters of Christian Charity. This plot of land was obtained by Father Koppernagle from Constantine Benitz, Mrs. Osler and the Young estate, at an outlay of $11,500.

Father Koppernagle started to build immediately and the completed building was dedicated September, 1878. During the four and one-half years that intervened between the passing of the deeds and the dedication of the church, there had been in progress a continuous church construction that, in uniqueness, probably has never had its counterpart in the United States.

WORK OF FATHER KOPPERNAGLE

We sometimes hear of a small mission church on the frontier or elsewhere built substantially by one man. But here was one of the largest churches in the city of

The great interior of St. Lawrence Catholic Church was put together by Father Clemens Koppernagle. (HSDC)

Harrisburg built entirely under the supervision and largely by the manual labor of the officiating priest. Father Koppernagle was his own contractor from start to finish. He drew the plans of the church and he minutely superintended and directed the work of the masons and the bricklayers he employed.

But if he was obliged to employ hired help on the exterior, the interior was all his own. Day by day, for years, alone and unassisted, he sawed and hewed and carved until creations of beauty stood forth beneath his chisel and mallet. The interior of the church is of pure Gothic style and very beautiful, and it was Father Koppernagle who did it all. He executed all the interior finish; the magic of his hand shaped the elaborate carving decorations. He did the window staining, made the pulpit and altars, formed the pews. He personally selected every piece of lumber and in the whole interior of St. Lawrence church, you cannot find a single defective or inferior stick. With Father Koppernagle the welfare of St. Lawrence congregation and the building for them of a suitable place for the worship of the Almighty had become a life work which absorbed his whole soul and being.

This grand old man died November 26, 1891, universally lamented, not by his own congregation or denomination alone, but by good citizens of every creed or of no creed at all who recognized in him that noblest work of God—a man honest in all the relations of life and faithful to the charge and talents entrusted to him.

LATER HISTORY OF ST. LAWRENCE

Father Koppernagle's successor was Rev. F.C. Seubert. After serving the congregation acceptably until July, 1899, Father Seubert was compelled to leave on account of ill health. He died at Elizabethtown in August of the following year.

The next rector at St. Lawrence was Rev. Stephen M. Wiest, a man universally popular with his parishioners, who was called away by death September 5, 1910. It was under Father Wiest's supervision that the frame buildings on Short street, used for the Parochial school, were replaced by an up-to-date brick building two stories in height, furnished with every necessary educational appliance. This was built in 1907. As already stated, Father Peter S. Huegel succeeded Father Wiest, and is the present competent and respected rector of St. Lawrence church.

BAND OF DEVOTED WOMEN

In 1885 a number of the Sisters of Christian Charity located here in connection with the St. Lawrence charge. Their first residence was at 113 Short street, the site of the present school building. Their home was subsequently changed to 107 Short street. They immediately took charge of the Parochial school which, however, had been in existence for some years previous to their advent. It had been up to 1895, under the care of August Karie, the organist at St. Lawrence and a musician of high repute.

6. Notable History of Wesley Union A.M.E. Zion Church

December 23, 1912

The Wesley Union A.M.E. Zion church at the corner of South and Tanner streets has the oldest continuous history of any church organization in the Park Extension district. The denomination had its origin in 1816. Prior to that time the colored Methodists of the United States were members of the same organization as their white brethren. A refusal of the Methodist Episcopal general conference to create a colored bishop to look specifically after the work amongst his own race led to a secession of a portion of the colored membership in the year above given. A division in the new denomination led to the branch now under consideration assuming the specific term "Zion" for all their churches, in contradiction to the term "Bethel" taken by the other branch. The latter denomination is also represented in the Park Extension district by the church at the corner of State and West streets.

There appears to have been a considerable number of members of the Zion church in Harrisburg from the very first, who associated themselves together. A formal organization, however, was not effected until August 20, 1829. The organization took place in a log building, located at Third and Mulberry streets, where there was, at that time, quite an extensive negro colony, the leading spirit amongst whom was the athletic and stately Mr. Bennett, generally known as "King" Bennett. For many years Mr. Bennett was the recognized chimney sweep of the town always having two or three little boys in his employ who did the actual work. Those were the days of wide chimneys and wood fires when every good citizen was expected to have his chimneys swept out at frequent intervals. If he neglected this, the borough authorities wanted to know the reason why. "King" Bennett was also an active agent of the celebrated "Underground Railroad," and many a poor fugitive was concealed in the houses at Third and Mulberry.

The year following the organization of the Harrisburg Zion church, the entire membership of the denomination in Pennsylvania was 841, of whom nearly one-seventh or 115, was in Harrisburg alone. In that year, 1830, the great David

Stevens, of Harrisburg, at the conference in Philadelphia, was ordained an elder and appointed to the Harrisburg circuit which comprehended the following preaching places: New Market, Chambersburg, Shippensburg, York, Swatara or Middletown, and Harrisburg. A goodly circuit that; and, in those days of very limited facilities of travel, it was no sinecure to get from point to point between those widely distant stations.

NOBLE BENEFACTOR OF COLORED RACE

Few men in Harrisburg have done as much to elevate the negro race as did the Rev. David Stevens during his long, honorable and self-sacrificing career. Some fifty years later he died, full of years and honor; and the membership of Zion church still justly revere the memory of one whose whole life was a continued succession of pious efforts and good deeds.

Under Stevens, the church membership grew so rapidly that it became necessary to lengthen the church sixteen feet. Stevens' successor in the pastorate, the Rev. Jacob D. Richardson, opened a school for colored children in the church. He did this partly to prevent the youth of his race from growing up in ignorance and partly because the poverty of his congregation was such that his pecuniary compensation as a minister was very inadequate. Under the Pennsylvania school law then in force the tuition of these poor children gathered into his school was paid by the county commissioners.

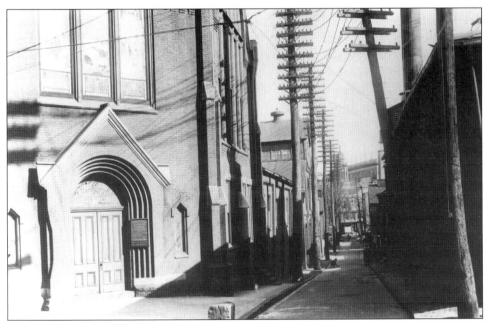

Wesley Union A.M.E. Zion Church stood on the corner of South Street and Tanner's Alley, where boys were playing marbles the day this photograph was taken. (HSDC)

The cornerstone on Wesley Union A.M.E. Zion Church reads 1895. (HSDC)

In November, 1832, however, Mr. Richardson was notified that, the Lancasterian building on Walnut street being in operation, his pupils must be sent there. Amongst those then transferred was Joseph B. Popel, afterwards a sanitary officer of the city. When, in 1879, the writer, as principal of the Boys' High School, admitted the Rev. William H. Marshall and John P. Scott to that school, there were sundry threats and much dissatisfaction on the part of some persons who were unaware, doubtless, of the fact that colored pupils had been freely admitted to the same building forty-seven years before.

Church in the Eighth Ward

So prosperous was the Wesley Union church that it became necessary to obtain larger quarters. At the same time the drift of the colored population had brought most of its members to the vicinity of its present location. Accordingly a lot was bought from the Forster estate, at Tanner and South streets, on which a small brick church was erected, facing Tanner street. To this new home the congregation removed November 24, 1839. The Rev. David Stevens was again the pastor. He had been the first and last in the old home and was now the first in the new.

In 1860 the church resolved to rebuild, but there was some delay on account of the excitement and uncertainties of the Civil War. The work, however, was begun in 1862, the building this time facing on South street. Whilst building, the congregation worshiped in a large old hall on Tanner street, commonly known as Bennett's hall. This stood about opposite the rear of the Citizen engine house and disappeared, through old age, many years ago. The first pastor in the new church was Rev. Abram Cole.

In 1886 this building was entirely remodeled, and, in 1894, the present commodious structure was erected, it being the third church building on the site in a space of 56 years. The pastor under whom this last church was built was the Rev. John F. Moreland, a very talented man, a close friend of President McKinley who, as Governor of Ohio, had appointed him to a responsible educational position. The officers of the church council under whom the building was carried forward were Henry S. Sigler, president, and John P. Scott, secretary. It is a commodious and well furnished church of substantial architecture. On one of the base stones are given dates which are prominent landmarks in the congregation's career, 1816, 1838, 1862, 1886, 1894.

One of the most prominent ministers of the past was the Rev. James A. Jones, pastor in 1858. The most distinguished member of the church during the more recent years was the Rev. Prof. William Howard Day, D.D., who was also its pastor in 1890. From that time on until his death he held responsible positions as a leading official of the general conference. Recently a monument was erected over his remains in Lincoln cemetery.

Some well known pastors of the past 20 years have been Rev. J.H. Anderson, Rev. William H. Snowden, Rev. James H. McMullen, Rev. Francis H. Hill, Rev. Martin L. Bialock, Rev. W.H. Ferguson and Rev. E.D.W. Jones. The present is Rev. Francis Lee.

The Zion congregation have already made full arrangements in regard to their new church home when the State shall take over their present property.

7. First Free Baptist Church:
Synagogue Kesher Israel

December 30, 1912

The Northeast corner of State and Fourth streets has been in use continuously for religious purposes since 1859, but, in that time it has been the property of three different sects.

What is now the Second Lutheran church of Harrisburg had its origins in a mission Sunday School founded January 11, 1855, by the S.S. Association of William Parkhill. A house was rented on East State street where the first Sunday School was held in a front room below.

So rapidly did the school increase that on the fourth Sabbath all the rooms on two floors were filled. In March, 1859, the lot at State and Fourth streets was leased and a chapel promptly built upon it which was surmounted by a small tower and a bell.

The Rev. C.A. Hay, of Zion church, preached here every alternate Sunday during the following winter. September 13, 1860, the congregation was regularly organized. The first pastor was the Rev. E.S. Johnston, who began his labors June 24, 1860. The first church officials were: Elders, Jacob Reel, D.A. Eyster; deacons, Charles Osman, Emanuel S. German, George Krichbaum, G.L. Murray. Soon after, the chapel was removed to William street and it is not germane to this article to follow the further migrations of the congregation until finally settled in their present home.

Secession from Fourth Street Church

Soon after the removal of the Lutheran chapel the lot was purchased by the newly formed First Freewill Baptist congregation who built a church upon it at an expense of $15,000. This congregation had its origin in a secession from the Fourth Street Church of God which was headed by the former pastor of the latter church, the talented Rev. James Calder, D.D. He was followed by a considerable number of the membership who were devotedly attached to him. The first services of the new congregation were held in the First Baptist church at Second and Pine streets.

The new church at Fourth and State streets was dedicated February 5, 1865. The Rev. James Calder continued in the pastorate until 1869, with the Rev. J.S. Burgess as an assistant from 1865 to 1868. After Mr. Calder the following pastors came in quick succession during a period of 13 years: The Rev. A.H. Chase, the Rev. A.F. Bryant, the Rev. Thomas Burkholder, the Rev. Thomas H. Drake and the Rev. William Fuller. Then Dr. Calder was back again for a few years with the congregation of his founding.

In the days of its vigor and activity the First Free Baptist church at State street also became the parent of another church. It has been stated that the Lutherans had removed their chapel to William and Calder streets. When, soon after, they chose another location, the First Free Baptist church had bought their chapel to use as a place to worship whilst their own church at State and Fourth was building. When it was no longer needed for this purpose, it was converted into a Baptist mission church and was known for many years after as the Third Free Baptist church.

DR. JAMES CALDER, NOTABLE MAN

Dr. James Calder was one of the prominent figures of Harrisburg during the last century. A man of profound erudition and a magnetic personality, he had hosts of enthusiastic friends and followers. He was for many years closely identified with the management and successes of State College. Amongst his sons well known in

The First Free Baptist Church stood on this corner at the turn of the century. The Bethel A.M.E. Zion Church is a few yards down the street. (HSDC)

our community were Captain Howard Calder, deceased, brave soldier, learned attorney and polished orator; and Russell Calder, holding a prominent position in the Pennsylvania steel works.

After Dr. Calder's second term of ministration to the church at State and Fourth streets its advancement was not as pronounced as it had been in the earlier years of its existence. Various causes retarded the church's development, one of which was that the location, no matter how well chosen at first, had ceased to be a convenient one for many of the membership. By degrees, the logic of events forced the conviction that a sale of the property would be desirable. From 1890 on the Rev. A.H. Shank, the Rev. Walter F. Cranston and the Rev. Thomas E. Brewster, in succession, ministered to the congregation.

HEBREW COLONIZATION IN THE EIGHTH WARD

In 1901 the First Free Baptist church found itself without a pastor. Meantime a mighty change had come over portions of the Ward as to the character of its population. For a decade before this large numbers of European Hebrews had been coming to Harrisburg. Many of these people were refugees from cruel persecutions in Russia where, in some cases, they had seen their loved ones slaughtered before their eyes. Many of them were very poor, but all possessed indomitable energy and industry. They toiled uncomplainingly at any work that came to their hands. Some were able to open small notion and grocery stores; some gathered junk and rags; some traversed wide areas with the peddler's pack on back and so on through all the diversified lines of industry open to willing hearts and ready hands.

Many of these poor folk who had attained the acme of their hopes and longings—refuge in the land where all stand equal in the light of freedom and opportunity—settled in the older portion of the Eighth Ward. They transformed whole sections of it, for as they purchased entire squares of property, former nests of infamy and gambling dens, which had once given East State street a wide notoriety, were extinguished or driven to other locations.

And as prosperity came in response to their toil, they desired suitable houses in which to worship God according to the manner of their fathers. One synagogue had already been located on Filbert street at the corner of North alley. October 1, 1902, the congregation Kesher Israel (spelled Kasher Israel on the front of the church) was organized.

Soon after, the Hebrews purchased the Baptist church, that organization realizing about the same amount as the original cost of the building and ground. This purchase price became the financial foundation of the new Baptist church at Fifteenth and Market streets.

The congregation Kesher Israel has prospered. The principal Rabbis have been Abraham Lassen; Nachman Heller, voluminous writer for the papers; and Louis Silver.

8. Bethel A.M.E. Church on State Street; Synagogue Chisuk Emuna; Christian and Missionary Alliance

January 6, 1913

Although not dating back quite as far in its organization as the Zion church on South street, the Bethel A.M.E. church on State street, is one of the old congregations of Harrisburg. For much more than a generation its membership worshiped on Short street below South right in the heart of the Park Extension district. As early as 1858 there was a flourishing congregation located at this point. The lot owned by the church was donated to it by a Mr. Stevens, who was a local minister of the denomination.

Stevens was a Lancaster lumber merchant doing quite an extensive business and was a man of considerable means, according to the rating of those days. On this lot two buildings were located in succession, the first being a log structure; the second, the frame building now used as an office by the Harrisburg Steam Heat and Power Company. This company bought the Short street church property for something like $2,500 when the congregation moved to their new edifice on State street, corner of West.

The State street lot was bought from William K. Alricks. The date stone in the base of the building gives 1891 as the date of its erection. It was a continuous work of several years, however, and it was not until 1894 that the interior work was finished and the church completely finished. The ground, building and furnishings represent an aggregate outlay, I understand, of approximately $23,000.

A list of the long line of pastors of this church organization would contain many names of the but dimly-remembered past and is scarcely necessary in an article like the present. One of the energetic ministers shortly before the erection of the new church was the Rev. Theodore Gould. Since the removal to State street the most prominent pastors in chronological order, have been the Rev. F.A. Smythe, the Rev. Solomon P. Hood, and the Rev. C.C. Dunlap. The present officiating minister is the Rev. J.H. Fickland.

Bethel A.M.E. Zion Church is to the left of West Alley in this photograph taken from the north side of State Street. (HSDC)

CHISUK EMUNA CONGREGATION

Chisuk Emuna was the first Hebrew religious body organized within the limits of the park extension. For several years services were held in a room on Walnut street, after which ground was purchased, and a neat frame synagogue erected at the corner of Filbert street and North alley. As the membership grew in numbers and prosperity, it was determined to have a more commodious and substantial place of worship. The present large brick synagogue on the site of the former frame building was the result.

A large hewn stone in the base of the synagogue gives the dates 5643 and 5668, respectively, for the organization of the congregation and the building of the present edifice. As the Hebrew chronology counts 3760 years from the creation to the beginning of the Christian era, these dates would be equivalent to 1893 and 1908 of our calendar.

Some of the leading rabbis in charge of the congregation since the first synagogue was erected on Filbert street have been Julius Kanter; Isman Notecoff; David Goldberg, the genial and well known interpreter; A. Rochman; H. Goldstein; Louis Silver; Solomon Murdick; and Isaac Minsky.

THE WRONG OF SLAVERY AND THE FOLLY OF PERSECUTION

Of the five stately places of worship within the limits of the park extension, four belong to people that have passed through some oppression. It is with special feelings of satisfaction that its writer has chronicled the history of the buildings that are monuments of their triumph over adverse circumstances.

It required the long hard logic of circumstances and the bitter blows of a cruel war to teach America that human slavery was debasing, not to the slave alone, but also to the master and the nation. The two colored churches in the Eighth Ward are trophies of the perseverance of a race whose pathway to the light of freedom's day was strewn with thorns and baptized with blood and tears. Through years of poverty, when every penny was won by toil, the membership consecrated a portion of their earnings that they might have suitable temples for the worship of the Almighty. And these temples to God have been bright oases in a Ward where there was much of sin. Through the influences emanating from them, hundreds have been led to lives of sobriety, honesty, and godliness.

CHRISTIAN AND MISSIONARY ALLIANCE

Besides the five churches described there have been, from time to time, within the limits of the park extension, a number of religious organizations occupying rented halls or residence buildings. The most prominent of these, in recent years, has been the Christian and Missionary Alliance, with headquarters at 513 North Fourth street. The principal pastors or superintendents in charge have been the Rev. C.D. Sawtelle, Dr. J.K. Smith, the Rev. J.S. Moore, and the Rev. F.H. Rossiter. A former location of the Alliance was on Sixth street, near Broad.

The most unique place of worship in the park extension district remains to be described in a subsequent article.

9. HARRY COOK AND LAFAYETTE HALL

JANUARY 13, 1913

From the churches of the Eighth Ward to Lafayette Hall, seems a far cry. Yet have I introduced Lafayette Hall here so that I can complete my description of buildings that have been used as places of worship. But it will be some time before I reach the religious part of Lafayette Hall's career.

No more spectacular character ever burst upon the horizon of the Eighth Ward than Harry Cook. Tall, well proportioned, handsome, of commanding appearance, a skillful dresser who produced unique effects by weird combinations of costly clothing, a ready and effective conversationalist, Harry Cook was a man bound to forge to the front in any rank in which he moved. Reared in a Christian home, a zealous church member to whom, even in early youth, responsible positions were assigned by his religious fellow workers, he yielded to other blandishments, forsook the God of his early covenant and allied his lot with others.

There have been as bad men in the Eighth Ward as Harry Cook. Undoubtedly, there have been worse men. There have been men from whom Harry Cook would have shrunk with abhorrence. But by common consent, the dashing Harry Cook stood forth as the typical and representative character of the element, a world to itself, that made the Eighth Ward of Harrisburg, forty years ago, notorious throughout the State. Old men of today, citizens and those who were then visitors here, may have forgotten all else about the Eighth Ward of the seventies of the last century, but one and all vividly recall Lafayette Hall.

On State street Cook built a mansion of brick intended to eclipse anything in his special line of business that had yet been seen in Harrisburg, and it did, architecturally. It was modeled after certain pretentious resorts of the day in New York. The basement was to be a restaurant; on the next floor was a barroom more elaborate with its massive marble bar and other ornate adornments than anything in the State outside of Philadelphia and Pittsburgh, and even those cities had few rooms fitted up with so utter a disregard of expense. Above this was to be a free-and-easy dance hall where most anything would go, and which was counted on to be a nightly money-maker of immense value. Connecting doors communicated

This 1917 photograph looking east from a capitol balcony shows much of the Eighth already demolished. The building facing State Street with the white outline may be Lafayette Hall. (PSA)

with the adjacent frame buildings under the same general management and specially presided over by Cook's wife.

Even the stable was a dream of art superior in construction to a majority of the dwelling houses of that day. In the stalls were costly mirrors and aught else in the aesthetic line that would be needed to make any reasonable horse contented with his lot.

But Harry Cook's schemes struck evil days. In the olden times, licenses for the sale of liquors were very easily obtained and inexpensive. The whole thing was largely a matter of form. Time was when low dens of infamy in the East State street section blazoned with alluring names.

But, about 1870, Harrisburg began to rally morally from the demoralization of Camp Curtin days. Churches and many business men banded together to produce better conditions. Amongst the young men who were foremost in the fight of that day were Samuel M. Sayford, the world-renowned evangelist, and Dauphin county's efficient Poor Director, Charles L. Boyer. Harry Cook soon ran afoul of the law and was deprived of his license by Judge Pearson.

More—the proprietor was pained to ascertain that the dance hall proposition was a little too advanced for Harrisburg. Reluctantly he withdrew what was to have been his greatest card. Still business, in various lines, around license-less Lafayette Hall and its annexes, was far from dull. The fools are never all dead at once. And the worst fools in the whole bunch are the gray headed fools and the bald headed fools that go into their second dotage and get giddy. And there was a fair share of that sort of suckers amongst Harrisburg's citizens and visitors forty years ago, just as today.

47

DEATH AND FUNERAL OF HARRY COOK

And then, unsummoned, the death angel came to the chamber of Harry Cook. With the appearance of that ghastly phantom, breaking in on him in the prime of manhood, came poignant memories of the life of rectitude which he had abandoned, the God whom he had despised. The scene at the death bed of Harry Cook, as told to me by a pious man who had been hastily summoned in his extremity, has never been told in print. I will not relate it now. If I ever do, it will be under the guise of a work of fiction.

The funeral of Harry Cook was as spectacular as had been his life. There was no stinting expense. The body of the man whose face, with its long, flowing silk-like whiskers, was yet handsome in death, was arrayed in the most gorgeous of his many suits of apparel.

A band headed the cortege which passed out State street and across the bridge to the Harrisburg cemetery. A long line of cabs followed, many of them filled with women of the underworld and Harrisburg's leading gamblers. It was an unofficial holiday in the "Eighth," for the street was densely lined with almost the entire colored population of the Ward.

And from many of these dusky onlookers came tears of genuine sorrow, for Harry Cook was no miser. He had a heart readily touched by tales of woe. He had given money lavishly to the poor and the needy. He had helped to bury the dead of these poor folk when men who would have considered Harry Cook's touch contamination had turned coldly away. No "down-and-out" had ever gone away hungry from Harry Cook's presence.

Harry Cook's monument stands in the middle of Harrisburg Cemetery. Beneath it lies a vault holding nine graves: Cook and his wife Hattie; Abraham and Mary Galebaugh and a much younger Abraham Galebaugh (probably not their son); Martin, Norman, and Elizabeth Shutt; and Jimmie Martin, who died at age 11.

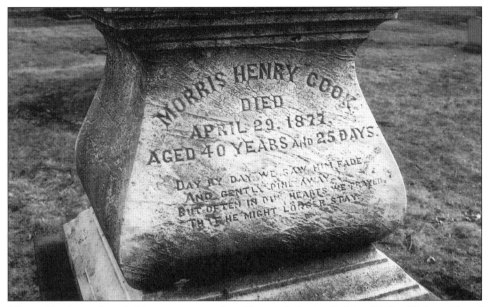

Harry Cook purchased this monument when Jimmie Martin died in 1872. All four sides of the monument are inscribed with the names of those buried there.

And may it not be that the tears of the poor who watched Harry Cook's funeral went high—very high—higher than any of us mortals know.

In Harrisburg cemetery, where the dust of the just and the unjust packed closely together, is commingled to nurture green grasses, flowery shrubs and luxuriant weeping willows, one of which shades the tomb of Harry Cook, his body was deposited. From a lot enclosed by heavy rails of corrugated steel welded into polished granite posts, rises a tasty monument, some 18 feet in height, bearing on one of its faces, the inscription:

> Morris Henry Cook, died April 29, 1877. Aged 40 years and 25 days
> Day by day, we saw him fade
> And gently pass away,
> But often in our hearts we prayed
> That he might longer stay.

Closely grouped about the monument are three smaller works of art, all very excellent in conception and faultless in execution. A number of the relatives of Cook's wife, including her father, are buried in the lot.

Thus, in one of the loveliest locations of well-kept Harrisburg Cemetery, Harry Cook awaits the last trump. God is his judge, not we. And well for us all that our Judge is an infinite and omniscient God, not finite and erring man.

The next number of this series will tell how Lafayette Hall became a house of prayer.

49

10. LAFAYETTE HALL RESCUE MISSION

JANUARY 20, 1913

In the year in which Harry Cook died and for many years before and after, there dwelt, in a substantial brick mansion on Walnut street near Fourth, a citizen named Kahnweiler. He was a thrifty man, and thriftiness had brought considerable means. His name was perpetuated for many years in "Kahnweiler's row," on Strawberry street below Fifth, but "Kahnweiler's row," is no more—the less is the pity. To Kahnweiler the proprietorship of "Lafayette hall" appeared to be about his size. He had built fairy air castles of the golden streams of profit to flow from this same proprietorship.

When a jolly Hibernian saw a bull (not a bull moose, but just a plain everyday bull) charging at him across a field, he was much amused at the animal's antics and laughed inordinately. A moment later when having been tossed across the fence, he picked himself from the ground, bruised and bleeding, he thus soliloquized, "Faith shure now! An' wasn't it well I had my laugh first?" So it was well for Kahnweiler that he had his golden dreams in advance. For many years he paid taxes on Lafayette hall, but not one penny of revenue did he ever derive therefrom.

The truth is Lafayette hall had become a white elephant and none realized that fact more quickly than did the widow of Harry Cook. So when she was offered a couple of good serviceable dwelling houses in exchange, the revenues from which would be sure and prompt, she had the best end of the bargain, although it took some years for the logic of events to hammer that idea into citizen Kahnweiler's head.

If Lafayette hall proved a failure for its builder it was still a greater one for its purchaser. The moral sense of the community, which had been somewhat blunted during and immediately after the Civil war, was rapidly rallying to higher ground.

STATE STREET RESCUE MISSION

For nearly a score of years after the death of its builder, Lafayette hall stood gaunt, dark, solitary and deserted. Its windows were roughly boarded up. Some colored folk along North alley told of uncanny sounds that came from it in hours of darkness—groans, shrieks and curses. Perchance the rats were holding high revel. Some even spoke of dancing lights and misty gliding figures that were dimly seen at the midnight hour. I know not.

There was a prominent citizen and business man of Harrisburg, a life long resident of our city, John W. Brown by name, whose home was at 210 Second street, and whose name will appear later as the proprietor of a foundry and machine works at State and Canal streets.

Daily, as Mr. Brown passed to and from his business place, he noted deserted Lafayette hall. For years he had been brought into contact with much of vice and poverty that was in startling evidence in the same vicinage. And from these two facts of daily observation gradually an idea was born in Mr. Brown's brain which took deep root and produced fruit. In conjunction with other Christian workers, men and women, Mr. Brown first opened up Lafayette hall to the light of day as a "Rescue Mission" and a home for the unfortunate and the erring.

There stood the marble bar as in days of yore, but the walls that once re-echoed to bald blasphemy and obscene jests, were now the scene of earnest prayer and melodious songs of praise. To make the contrast between the past and the present the more emphatic, the cobwebbed whisky bottles which had stood in their accustomed places through all the years of the room's desolation, were allowed to remain through those other years that it resounded nightly with exhortation—a

Lafayette Hall was just a few doors down State Street from this intersection with Cowden Street. Lewis Baturin's establishment is across the street from the McCarthy House. (HSDC)

silent, but most eloquent and ever present testimonial of the changes time had wrought in the building which had been erected to be Harrisburg's most gorgeous palace of sin.

The magnificent stable was converted into a wood house in which the needy wanderers taken into the mission prepared kindling which was sold throughout the city. In this and in many other things the mission followed the methods of the rescue homes of the Salvation Army.

So interested was John W. Brown in the works of the mission that, at times, when no suitable superintendent could be obtained, he himself assumed the duties of that position, he having retired from an active business life a few years before. The Superintendent before Mr. Brown was S.J. Caskey. Subsequently the duties of the office were discharged for some years by J.M. Cuswin.

LAFAYETTE HALL A BUSINESS PLACE

September 1903, the then new Paxtang Electric Co., with a plant at the southern end of the city, turned on its lights in Harrisburg, and 512 State street became its station for supplies.

Lafayette hall is rapidly becoming a misty memory, but the evil things it stood for still exist in our community, although not so glaringly courting the light of publicity. And yet there have been, in very recent years, licensed hotels, right in the heart of Harrisburg, that, in licentiousness and bestiality, were very little short of Lafayette hall in its palmiest days.

In all attainments for civic good eternal vigilance is the price of safety for the Salvation of the sons and daughters growing up in our homes.

The fine building at the end of Short Street is Harrisburg Technical High School, formerly the Lancasterian School, and now Old City Hall Apartments. (HSDC)

11. Public Schools in the Park Extension

January 27, 1913

The only public school building within the limits of the Capitol Park extension is the one on North street, erected in 1876, which was known for many years as the "Lincoln" building. Recently, when it was the wish of the school authorities to give that name to one of the large new school buildings on Allisons hill, the North street building was rechristened the "Day" school house. No more appropriate name could have been given it. Rev. Prof. William Howard Day, D.D., was, by all odds, the greatest man of the colored race who ever resided in Harrisburg. The welfare of his people was close to his heart, and he did more to elevate and improve them than any one man of our municipality. For many years, in the Harrisburg Board of School Control, where he was a power, the building on North street was ever under his watchful eye. With its disappearance, it is to be hoped that the name of this great educator and representative men of the colored race will not be eliminated from the nomenclature of Harrisburg's school edifices. For one year (1904) the school house on North street was known officially as the "Burns" building. Then the term disappeared from the roster. Daniel S. Burns certainly did enough for the schools of Harrisburg to have his name perpetuated in one of our school buildings.

The "Day" building contained several large rooms and has always been devoted entirely to colored pupils. Previous to its erection, the provision for the negro scholars of the Eighth Ward was extremely crude. On South street, in the rear of the Jennings foundry, was a large frame edifice occupying the space between the foundry and the Zion A.M.E. church. It stood there, rather dilapidated, during the latter years of its career, until demolished to make way for the Newby building erected in 1895.

This three-story frame building was universally known as "Franklin Hall," and was applied to a multiplicity of uses. In it met the colored secret, beneficial and temperance societies of the olden time. Here were held festivals and church fairs. Religious organizations that had no other home rented rooms in it. Political

The Lincoln School, on the south side of North Street near Fifth. It was later renamed the William Howard Day School, in recognition of the first black president of the Harrisburg School Board, who served in that office from 1891 to 1893. The school system was generally segregated, however, and this building was for African-American students only. The flag has 48 stars, so the photograph must have been taken in 1912 or later. (PSA)

meetings were held there at such times as the bosses thought it incumbent on them to enthuse the colored brethren about the duty of voting the whole ticket.

Amidst its other uses the colored pupils of the Eighth Ward were housed in certain rented rooms of Franklin Hall, 421 South street. The accommodations were of the poorest; the rooms were destitute of apparatus or even ordinary school room conveniences, whilst to sanitary and hygienic precautions not a thought was given. It was, therefore, a great change for the better when the pupils of the Franklin building, which was officially known as the "Jennings" school, were transferred to the new edifice in North street, which was quite an up-to-date structure according to ideas on school architecture thirty-six years ago.

In the earlier days of our public schools no provision had been made for the training of colored teachers. Consequently, it being difficult to obtain qualified men and women of that race, white teachers were often employed in colored schools. A conspicuous example was John A. Krause, a prominent citizen of the past generation, who taught for many years, in the "Jennings" building and was transferred to North street in 1877, remaining there until 1858 [?] when, enfeebled by the slow approach of insidious disease, he was unable longer to teach. Other teachers in the "Jennings" building back in the early seventies of the last century were George H. Imes, a colored citizen who once announced himself as a candidate for the Republican nomination for Lieutenant Governor; Ellen E. Johnson; John Shoop; and Susan E. Herbert.

TEACHERS IN NORTH STREET SCHOOL

The first supervisory principal of the schools in this building was Spencer P. Irvin, a teacher of great ability. He it was who prepared the first colored pupils for the High school. Amongst the number were two prominent citizens of today, Prof. John P. Scott and Rev. William H. Marshall. So thoroughly did he do this work that their examination was one of the most brilliant ever recorded in Harrisburg of grammar school pupils applying for admission to the High School. Mr. Irvin was determined to leave no loop-hole for invidious comparison in regard to the first colored scholars who would be brought in direct scholastic competition with the white students of the city.

In 1882 Morris H. Layton succeeded Mr. Irvin as supervisory principal, a place he has occupied ever since. Mr. Layton had been a teacher in the building from the time it was opened in 1877, so that he has an unbroken teaching record of 35 years in the one location.

The other teachers in the "Day" school, strewn along the more than one-third of a century of its existence, have been Annie E. Casmond; Henrietta V. Potter; Conlissa L. Lyons; Florence Robinson, daughter of former park policeman David Robinson; Florence M. Smith, who began her work in 1882 and taught there for ten consecutive years; John Powell Scott; Annie M. Cooper; Annie Summers; Julia A. Johnson; Marguerite E. Wilhams; James Stuart, a talented high school graduate, who after a few years of successful work was cut down by death whilst in the prime of early manhood; Ida E. Brown; J. Henry Williams; Clara E. Reed; Florence M. Bradley; Helen Taylor; and Alice E. Price.

Mr. Scott became a teacher immediately after his graduation in 1882 and is still in the business. As the increase of colored pupils necessitated the opening of more schools for them than could be accommodated in the North street building, Mr. Scott was moved in 1898 to the DeWitt building and when that was set apart for the Technical high school, to the Wickersham. At a later period, J. Henry Williams was transferred to the same building, whilst Miss Marguerite Wilhams also taught there for a time.

A prominent feature of the "Day" building for a number of years has been the excellent work of Miss Ida E. Brown, daughter of the well-known citizen, Cassius M. Brown, and Miss Clara E. Reed, both meritorious graduates of our well adjusted public school system.

The janitors at North street have been Joseph B. Pople, 1877–1882; John Napper; Robert Young, 1886–1899; Henry Butler; James H. Hunter, an ex-policeman and at one time a prominent factor in Eighth Ward politics; and John H. Lee.

Once on a time there was in the Eighth Ward, a little public school, of very pleasant memories which will be noticed briefly in the next number of this series.

12. Public Schools in the Park Extension (continued)

February 3, 1913

While the colored children of the Eighth Ward were packed, like sardines in a box, in the uncomfortable and unsanitary rooms of the "Jennings" school, at Franklin Hall, 421 South street, the Harrisburg school board found it incumbent upon them to make some provision for the little white girls of the district, who were too small to be sent to the more distant buildings attended by the older white pupils. Accordingly a one story frame shop, adjacent to the Mt. Vernon Fire Company's home, was rented.

Back in the early seventies of the last century Miss Kate B. Casey was the teacher. Upon her death in 1878, Miss Adelaide F. Gotta became the teacher. The instructor from 1881 to 1883 was Miss Grace E. Walters; from 1883 to 1886, Miss Lulu Crane. In the latter year, Miss R. Emma Coleman took charge of the school, remaining there until, in 1879, it was transferred to the newly erected Wickersham building at the corner of Cowden and Briggs streets. The janitors at this school during the last quarter of a century of its existence were H.W. Scott, Mrs. Mary Wennell for a term of three years, Sarah Sides for eight years, Sarah Buffington for five years, Mrs. Rebecca Colsher, and Mary Shiffler during the last year.

For many years the little one-room school was known only as the Fourth street building, but, soon after the assassination of President Garfield, his name was given to it. It was in some respects the most unique school that ever existed in Harrisburg. It was a world all in itself to the little tots, who attended it, unmarred by any big boys or big girls. All the young ladies who have been mentioned as presiding over the school were affectionate and lovable, and on them the wee girls of this little world lavished the wealth of their affection.

It is a sight to melt the heart of a stoic to see the wee tots gather in front of the school room door of a pleasant morning watching for the appearance of the teacher. As soon as she was seen in the distance, there was a rush to meet her, and she would be escorted to the school room with twenty or more guileless children

Across the street from the Brotherly Love Lodge on the north side of South Street, at 421 South, was the Jennings School for "colored" students, also known as Franklin Hall. (PSA)

pressing close around her, each one striving to get nearest. Many a matron will read this sketch to whom will be recalled the happy school days of a fourth or third of a century ago when they were of the bevy of happy hearts that met daily for delightful school work in the old frame shop.

After the little building ceased to be a school room it had a multiplicity of uses. For some years past it was the office and work shop of Contractor Stuckey. It has now been purchased by the State and has disappeared from history forever.

BOATING DAYS

Before completing this series I intend to say something of every industrial plant now in existence in the park extension district, tracing each one through its successive occupancies. But now I want to tell of some big business places, once running with life, that disappeared before the present generation was born.

When canals were dug through the State, before railroads existed, they became a mighty factor in solving transportation problems of that day. With Harrisburg as a principal point on one of these artificial waterways, business of every kind in the borough received a boom. Large warehouses were built along the canal which received the freight brought here in boats and distributed it to customers in Harrisburg and the adjacent region. These warehouses and general stores along the canal dealt in almost every conceivable article, the many boatmen who were passing daily and who were very free, as a general rule, in spending the money earned on the towpath.

It is not the design of the writer to trace all the warehouses that arose and flourished in the present Eighth Ward. Nor would it be profitable to do so. The place they occupied has long since been gridironed with railroad trackage and consequently is not strictly within the bounds of the present park extension. Yet their existence is so closely allied with the development of this portion of the Eighth Ward that a full history of the district demanded some brief allusion to them.

In 1865 there were three leading business places, of the kind described above, along the Eighth Ward section of the canal. There were Gross & Kunkle, with warehouse, store and wharf on Canal street, between State and Walnut; Levi Weaver & Co. on Canal street foot of Walnut, who confined themselves to groceries, flour, feed and provisions; and Red & Co., on Canal street at the foot of State, who combined with the forwarding and commission business a very extensive wholesale and retail grocery trade.

Some of these houses under various ownerships had been in existence then for a quarter of a century; and new ones arose, from time to time, until the day came that the canal could no longer compete with the railroad, and then they passed out of being.

The influence which the canal, whilst in its prime, had in the development of the present park extension district will be told in the next number of this series.

At the east end of State Street is the stone-ramped, iron State Street Bridge over the Pennsylvania Railroad tracks and the Pennsylvania Canal. (HSDC)

13. The Tow Path Men and Lumber Raft "Yankees" Who Infected the Eighth Ward

February 10, 1913

The section subsequently known as the Eighth Ward was not thickly populated in the canal boating days prior to the Civil war. Even during that conflict and, for some years after, it was far from presenting the congested condition of more recent years. There were along State street and to an even greater extent on North street considerable stretches of vacant lots.

To this statement of a rather sparse population in the earlier days of its history, one exception must be taken. Parts of what is now the "Eighth" had early become a haven of refuge for a large colored population, many of them very poor, some fugitives from southern slavery who lived in daily dread of being recognized and hauled back to bondage.

A prominent citizen of Harrisburg, whose recollection goes back very clearly to the year 1840, tells me that at that time there was a large colored population on Tanner, Short and South streets and the adjacent alleys. This settlement extended down as far as the line of Cowden, which had not then been laid out as a street.

But we have historical evidence of a large colored element in this section yet fifteen years earlier. There have been several serious riots in Harrisburg, covering a long period of years, in consequence of attempts to recapture fugitive slaves. The earliest of these was April 21, 1825. On this occasion a large crowd of colored men and boys made a desperate effort to take the poor fugitive from his owner and the officers of the law.

The record tells us that they came streaming in hot haste, to the conflict from Tanner, Short and adjacent streets, a tumultuous crowd. The finale was not a very satisfactory one for the colored men. They were unsuccessful in releasing the fugitive and sixteen of the mob were arrested. When placed on trial twelve were convicted, one of whom was subsequently successful in giving leg bail. The other eleven went to the tread-mill, one of the cherished adjuncts of civilization a century ago, which the borough of Harrisburg had built some time before at an expense of $300.

HOW CANAL BUILT UP THE EIGHTH

But with all the increase of business which the canal brought to the Eighth Ward section, it was but natural that it should also add somewhat to its population. And those additions were not altogether of a desirable class. It has been a common impression that the houses of ill fame and gambling dens, which long gave the "Old Eighth" an unenviable notoriety, were a product of war days. The era of the Civil war only tended to increase the excrescences. They had their origin and had attained a flourishing growth anterior to Camp Curtin times.

And right here let it be said, parenthetically, that no history of the park extension district would be a full one that did not recognize the existence of vice conditions which long held sway over considerable portions of that territory and yet continue in some parts of it. But let no one fall into the error of thinking that all the population was a depraved one. There have been at all times, a large number of honest, industrious, upright, God-fearing men and women in the Old Eighth Ward, who have reared their families in the paths of virtue and rectitude. Harsh conditions have often compelled them to dwell close to dens of depravity. All the more honor to these people, white and black, who have maintained a life of rectitude. That vice at one time, held high revel in the "Eighth" was due to

This undated view from the State Street Bridge over the Pennsylvania Canal shows the north end of the Eighth Ward, the Howard Eby Coal and Wood Company, and a rare scene of a canal boat full of men. (HSDC)

some extent to the laxity of some civic administrations in a rigid enforcement of the law. But back of this there was a callousness of public opinion. It required many years for the mass of the body polite to recognize the fact that a plague spot in any one locality is a fearful menace to the mass of the body politic.

The men who followed the tow path sixty years ago were not generally the men who sought out a prayer meeting when they tied up for the night. Hence there arose hotels and worse—which sought to cater to the boatmen and to win from them their hard-earned dollars. Nearly every licensed place of the section had a room set apart for gambling. But the gambling dens of the bellum and ante-bellum days were not confined to licensed saloons. Half a century ago and more gambling was well nigh a national vice, which permeated every strata of society from the most brilliant statesmen of congressional halls down to the laborers with pick and shovel who were excavating our railway beds.

But the canal boatmen were not the only patrons of the cheap and gaudy resorts that sprang up along East State street, Canal street and adjacent thoroughfares.

THE UP-RIVER "YANKEES"

The "Yankees" who came down with the spring rafting season heard there was something doing over canalway, and did not propose to let the boatmen have all the fun. The "Yankees" made everybody in Harrisburg aware of their presence. There was no mock modesty about these fellows. For months they wrought laboriously amidst primeval solitudes. But one and all looked forward to the one holiday period of the year when, with the spring freshets, they would take their rafts to the lower Susquehanna and be paid off at Havre de Grace, or Columbia, or Wrightsville. And then they lost little time in making tracks for the nearest town that had something doing. Many of them made Harrisburg their objective point for a seance with the various phases of sin prior to their departure for another long era of cutting and logging. When here they made it a point to concentrate in a continuous session of twenty-four or forty-eight hours practical experience in every form of wickedness the town could ladle up. And yearly, those of the town, male and female, who had any brand of sin on tap, ready for delivery, waited impatiently for the advent of the upriver "Yankee" and his coin.

They were, too, like the boatmen, a tribe to be handled with caution, for if they started rough house, it did not take them many minutes to clear out a bar room or gambling shack, furniture, occupants and all. On the other hand, if they wanted into a place that was barred against them, they resorted to the simple expedient of kicking in the panels of the door with a dozen pair of toughest cowhide boots simultaneously applied. Should the oak prove too massive and the bolts too firm, an ax in the deft hands of one of these hardy woodmen would send door, bolts, locks, chains, staples and clasps inward in one whirling mass.

The "Yankees" in their season, assisted the canal men in preparing the park extension district for the yet more unsavory fame awaiting it in Camp Curtin days.

14. The Park Extension Section in Civil War Days: How "Bounty Jumpers" Were Handled in the East State Street Dens

February 17, 1913

But all that canal boatmen and lumber raft "Yankees" had been able to do in the way of rendering the present park extension district a lively place became insignificant before the revels that characterized that section in Civil War days. With Camp Curtin located here, for four years troops, troops, troops were coming and going in numbers such as this Western continent had never known. Often there were 10,000 and more in camp. For four years money circulated in Harrisburg as ceaselessly as the flow of water through reservoir pipes. There were men here with money to burn and a burning desire to spend it; for they dreamed that the golden stream, or more accurately the greenback stream would never cease.

There were maids of the town and matrons, too, whose husbands were at the front, who were willing to assist in the depletion of plethoric pocketbooks. And their sisters came to the banquet from distant towns, for the news had gone forth over the land that Harrisburg was one of the greatest of war camps, and hither the buzzard of prey, male and female, hastened.

What is now the Eighth Ward did not hold all the deviltry of the day, but its resorts were pre-eminent in evil odor. To them the wild young blades of the camp, freed from the shackles of home restraint, poured forth by legions, seeking dissipation, and they found it, each day, furnishing a fruitful calendar of crime, and blasphemy, and debauchery. There were orgies by day, and fiercer orgies by night that were protracted till the stars had paled before the brightening eastern skies.

Sunday was a red letter day in the dens of East State and Canal streets. Then drink flowed in maddening swirls until the surging crowds of the barrooms,

An Underground Railroad "station" was located on Tanner's Alley in the 1850s. (HSDC)

bursting open the doors, transferred to the vacant lots around and the swamps beyond the railroad tracks, the brutal fights commenced within.

Harrisburg had many places during the Civil war reeking with darksome episodes and malodorous memories, but none that were blacker or more law defying than the resorts of what was subsequently the Eighth Ward. In regard to some of these places there were persistent rumors that would not drown of deeds of foul play; and there were shacks where, in after years, rumor claimed that the victims would enchannel themselves in the midnight hours, and would stalk in uncanny forms through the halls of their former orgies. 'Twas said there were dancing lights that moved from room to room, and groans and shrieks such as might send eerie creeps over the stoutest of hearts.

For many following years there were around our city flotsam and jetsam, storm-tossed wreckage, on life's sea, that dated from Camp Curtin days and from wild debaucheries, which had lost their merriment and left only maddening serpent stings of anguish. Ten years later there were women who, when the war began, were beautiful girls and the light of happy homes in Harrisburg and other towns all over our land, that were wrinkled and haggard old women detesting life and fearing to die. For in Harrisburg, then and now, as surely as when St. Paul wrote to the Romans, "The wages of sin is death."

"BOUNTY JUMPERS" OF 1864

As volunteering came to a standstill and immense levies of recruits were demanded to replenish the ranks devastated by battle and disease, drafting was

This 1904 photograph shows unpaved Tanner's Alley, looking south. (PSA)

resorted to. To avoid the draft, citizens of the various municipalities offered enormous bounties for recruits to fill their quotas. And then the professional "bounty jumper" was born. They abounded in Harrisburg and furnished fat picking for the gamblers and crooks who handled them. The headquarters of the various gangs and the principal points from which they were handled were a number of locations of shady repute along the railroad tracks and in the East State street vicinage.

There was one den on East State street in particular that did a big business in defrauding both the government and the bounty jumping tool; for, as a general rule, the "bounty jumper" got but a small share of his dishonestly acquired money. Say he received $500, his manager, located at the East State street joint, would take about $400 as his charges for handling him, putting him in, securing connivance at his immediate desertion, and providing a safe harborage for him.

These managers claimed that at least $200 had to be paid to men connected with the camp. In this, perchance, they sometimes lied to their tools, for they were all a precious set of cut-throats and villains together. Doubtless they often told the substantial truth, for, by 1864, nearly every department of the government had become permeated with noisome, festering corruption.

While a million men were fighting and many thousands were dying for the union, there were thousands who were defrauding the government and defrauding the nation's soldiers of what was their due, and thus laying the foundation for colossal fortunes. Rotten provisions were sold to the United States at full price and passed by bribed inspectors; medical stores were stolen by the ton from field hospitals and resold to the government.

The catalogue is a long one for the canker of greed had eaten deep. Had there been no corruptible officials in higher or subordinate positions, bounty jumping could have been broken up in twenty-four hours in Harrisburg, Albany and every recruiting center.

Well, the tool in the case being allowed to retain $100 of the $500 he had received (and he was under constant and danger-fraught espionage till he paid over the $400), the great aim of the men who used him was to separate him from that $100 as quickly as possible.

There were several means of accomplishing this. The most common and safest was the gaming table. As soon as the tool had made his getaway from Camp Curtin, he would report to his East State street headquarters for concealment in case there was an attempt at pursuit. Each one of these places had a gambling room presided over by one or more expert blacklegs. As soon as the deserter had reported at the rendezvous, he would be plied with liquor and induced to gamble. Generally he had no objection to either form of dissipation.

The next morning the man had not one penny of the $500, and was dependent upon the vipers who had him in tow for the advance of a little money till they saw a chance to put him in to jump another bounty.

It was an endless chain with the poor dupe always in the position of the empty bucket. The sharpers got the money. All the "bounty jumper" ever earned or had to show for his infamous acts was an eternity of shame.

I never knew or heard of a professional bounty jumper that was not a dead beat and a bum for the rest of his life, for a man that got that low had seared from his soul any particle of manhood that might ever have been in it.

How shameful the business was is evinced by the fact that, in all our broad land, not one man can be found who is willing to stand up and say, "I was a bounty jumper." In fact, most of them are dead now, for they were not the breed of animals that would live very long. They had too many meannesses to be liable to longevity.

Some of the frame gambling shacks of the East State street vicinage that were bounty jumper stations were replaced years ago by improved buildings as the advent of a new element in the Ward began to elevate portions of it to a higher plane. All will disappear soon beneath the leveling operations of the State's agents.

The bounty jumpers and the crooks who handled them have disappeared yet more rapidly than the buildings in which they operated, so that now they are but a misty memory. The sharp manipulators who managed the dupes profited not by their ill gotten gains, and generally died dependent on the charity of others. A notorious gambler, who at one time claimed that he had handled two hundred bounty jumpers from dens of the East State street section, ended life as a pauper.

15. Old Time Gambling Dens of the Park Extension Section

February 24, 1913

When the first gambling dens were opened in what is now the Eighth Ward, for the especial accommodation of canal boatmen and lumber raft "yankees," it was at a time when gambling was almost regarded as a legitimate occupation, when many legislators, congressmen and statesmen of high position were inveterate gamesters and lost little caste by being so known. This quasi-respectability was the most insidious and deadly feature of this national vice of ante-bellum days.

At the time when the rough gambling houses of the park extension district began their career, there were faro banks at the corner where the Grand Opera House was subsequently erected; the next door Sanfords theatre on part of the present Star Independent site; on Market street immediately west of where Eby's grocery was afterwards built; on a portion of the site where subsequently stood the Gross House, and then the Hotel Columbus; on the south side of Locust street, not far from Second; and at other places in the heart of the borough. The existence of these places was generally known to officials and citizens, many of whom patronized them liberally. There was no attempt at concealment of the business carried on in these places.

During all the years before and during the war and for a considerable time after, there was no honest, continuous effort on the part of the authorities to close them. Spasmodic informations generally took the form of bleeding the faro proprietor whose bank account was supposed to be fat. When he came down, as he had to, the case disappeared. If strangers lost their money in gambling resorts and squealed, they generally got a much severer dose than the gamblers. So victims soon learned it was wisdom to hold their tongues.

Such being the conditions in the business and resident sections of the city, it was not to be expected that the rough joints which sprang up between the Capitol buildings and the canal in a part of the city to which the scanty police force of that day seldom penetrated would be seriously molested. The Eighth Ward gambling dens differed only from the more aristocratic resorts in the heart of the town in

The rear of 406 Walnut Street, The Out Let store, shows that even in a poor neighborhood, the balcony woodwork could be attractive. (PSA)

being conducted by a more desperate set of men, who would stop at no crime necessary to plunder their victims.

The men who patronized these dens of the olden time in the East State street vicinage were generally a rough set. Legislators and well-to-do citizens, generally, fought shy of them. But occasionally a resident or more frequently a casual visitor to the Capitol city in search of excitement, and possessed of more money than sense, would enter the doors of an East State street gambling den. What the accomplished blacklegs of the place would do to their victim of this class, was always a-plenty. He always left minus his money, and thoroughly dazed from drugged drinks. He was indeed lucky if part of his clothing had not been appropriated.

EAST STATE GAMBLING DENS

But it was with the opening of Camp Curtin that gambling and other evil resorts of the Eighth Ward section blossomed out into their full career of crime, just as similar places became more active in other portions of Harrisburg. The East State places, however, seemed to sound a profounder depth of depravity and thus acquired a State-wide notoriety, which has only ceased to exist in more recent years.

With the influx of tens of thousands and the lavish payment of money connected with military matters, all that Harrisburg had known of gambling was eclipsed. The faro banks were worked overtime and new ones sprang up. But the low haunts generally connected with a disreputable drinking place (for almost anyone could get a license then for almost any kind of a place) acquired increased vitality. Those of the State and Canal street sections hummed with life. A man had little chance in the faro rooms; in the lower dens he had none.

A Mountaineer's Experience

How things were done in these dens is best told by a concrete example. In the company the writer assisted in bringing to Camp Curtin in 1864, was a goodly sprinkling of mountaineers. Amongst these was a certain man named William (last name immaterial) who had a weakness for cards and was the champion at "old sledge" of all the district around his mountain home. But draw poker was his especial fondness.

William had cleaned out everybody living in the mountains between Adams and Franklin counties, Penna., that had tackled him at cards. He sighed for new worlds to conquer. In fact, I suspect that the flag and the preservation of our glorious Union had not such a sight to do with William's enlistment. It is probable that next to the $500 bounty, the strongest inducement to William in donning the blue and contracting to eat Uncle Sam's hardtack and pork, was the fact that it would take him to pastures new where, doubted not, there were suckers to be gulled.

William lost no time in striking out to make his fortune. It was September 4, 1864, when he was paid his $500 bounty. That happened to be Sunday, for in September, 1864, there was no Sabbath day observance worth bragging about in Camp Curtin, and not much, truth to tell, in any part of Harrisburg outside of the church edifices. William, like a thrifty soul sent $400 home. Would not $100 be ample capital to boost him into the Vanderbilt class, if judiciously invested in skinning the victims that would come his way.

The next day William started out to find a game. He found it with surprising ease. He found a friend to humanity, who knew where there was a wicked nest of gamblers on State street, near Canal, who could be cleaned out neatly if the right man went up against them. William had a hunch that he was the right man. As they trod the classic pavements of East State street, the friend to humanity suggested that they "likker up." Now William had rather a weakness for liquor, especially when someone else paid for it. So they "likkered up" on some of the concentrated poison that the East State street dens of that day served to their victims. In fact they "likkered" several times. William now felt cocksure that he was the man to clean up those disreputable gamblers and drive them into some honest employment.

When they entered the shack that was their destination, the game looked good to William and he sailed in. At first he won some small amounts. William was not at all surprised. He knew things would come his way.

THE END OF WILLIAM'S GAME

Then things happened, but how William never exactly knew; and in about ten seconds his $100 was gone. The mountaineer leaped three feet in the air, cracked his army brogans together, shook his brawny fists at the other players and inquired, by the great horn spoon, what they supposed he was there for? He had been "honswoggled" (whatever that is) and he could thrash the "honswogglers" and a ton of wild cats beside.

What was done to William in the next few minutes is painful to contemplate. It was also very painful to William. It is a sad commentary on human nature that the friend to humanity who had steered William to the joint, assisted actively in doing him up.

When William next became interested in mundane affairs, he was on the broad of his back in an alley. His clothing was torn; his flesh was lacerated—likewise his feelings and his trust in human nature. He was an assorted and miscellaneous

East of the intersection of Walnut Street and Tanner's Alley, the business of the corner store, The Out Let Clothing Manufacturing Company, is evident. (HSDC)

collection of hurts and bruises. He had no time to make an inventory of his pains. They were too numerous. He felt as if he was a whole hospital Ward; and found himself wondering, as he gazed up at the sky, whether a half dozen battles down in old Virginia would be more disastrous.

His first thought, when he finally got in motion, was "to likker up" but he didn't have the price of a "likker-up" in his clothes. William hied himself to Camp Curtin and made lurid moan to his company officers. They curtly told him to stay away from such places. He tried to find the camp commandant whose duty he supposed to be to right all wrongs. But an unfeeling guard told him it was the colonel's busy day.

Then William tried to rouse his fellow mountaineers to rise in their right and raid the "cussed gambling-hole," leaving no vestige of it unless his $100 was forthcoming. But many of these mountaineers had felt William's sharp fangs in games of the past, and, rejoicing at his plight, they simply gave him the laugh.

So, when a few days later, William marched across "the Camelback," penniless, sore in body and distressed in mind, he felt that he had a return game to play on East State street, Harrisburg, and he would, if not shot in Virginia, keep the engagement.

The next number of this series will tell how East State street welcomed William to the return game.

At 434 Walnut Street, on the northwest corner of Walnut and Short Streets, sat the Harrisburg Cash and Carry Grocery, featuring a traditional delivery wagon. (PSA)

16. Old Time Gambling Dens of the District: The Mountaineer's Return Game

March 4, 1913

The William from Camp Curtin whose sad experience in an East State street gambling den was narrated in last number, amid Virginia mud and marshes, never lost sight of the sweet revenge he hoped to have "when the cruel war was over." At length the time arrived "when Johnny came marching home;" and William, with the assistance of hugging a hospital cot whenever the doctor would permit it, had managed to dodge all the bullets.

Again the cattle cars discharged their freight of packed humans over on the Wormleysburg shore; and again William's hoofs stirred up the accumulated dust of decades in the old "Camelback." Harrisburg was swarming with gamblers, cutthroats, pickpockets and every variety of thieves and thugs. They came from many cities. So desperate were they in their scent after plunder that they even invaded "Camp Return" where long lines of soldiers were being paid off continuously day and night.

One hunchbacked pickpocket from the purlieus of New York city was kicked to death—to a shapeless jelly, in the twilight of one morning's early dawn as he tried to ply his vocation on the "Ridge road" just outside the camp gates.

The boys in blue for greater safety would start together from camp for the trip to the depots in squads of fifteen or twenty. When his acquaintances asked William to join them, he had a faraway look in his eyes, and a dry, sarcastic smile wreathed his lips as he replied:

"No, I'm not goin.' I'll jist loaf around Harrisburg a day or so."

William's Second Visit

[missing or garbled words] . . . and now badly dilapidated building in the last square of East State street, before reaching the canal, right within the shadow of the present State street bridge is a building, soon to be destroyed, which was the location in 1865, of the very toughest gambling joint and resort for all-round deviltry of this whole malodorous section, and thither William wended his way.

He took a couple of drinks incidentally announcing that "at old sledge he could beat the man made the Keards." Now the person who irrigated himself with the condensed lightning which was sold in East State street, during war days, was liable to be fit for any deed of lunacy five minutes thereafter.

As a matter of accommodation to William he was taken into an inner room, where he was introduced to three gentlemen who, with himself, could make up a nice quiet little game. Now, these men were very full of business, for the town was very full of suckers. So they did not propose to waste any unnecessary time on William. But one set of hands had been dealt, when, as the cards were lifted from the table, one of the trio broke out in an exclamation of disgust. "Why couldn't this thing have been poker?" He had quite a nice thing in poker and now the hand was simply wasted in a seven-up game.

The same thought had already occurred to William as he saw four kings staring him in the face. He bit instantly. He bit good and hard, just as the confederates had intended he should. He kept on biting till every penny of his four months' earnings from Uncle Sam, lately handed to him by Paymaster Baird, were on the table. Then four aces were flashed before his eyes and the money disappeared.

How William Dodged the Engines

William started to raise a row and a blackjack put him out of the fighting game yet more quickly than he had gone out of the game of combined old sledge and poker. When darkness fell he was carried out and thrown along the railroad tracks. William actually tried to pray, and I guess it was the first time in his life, as he went crawling around dodging engines and freight trains.

Policemen were not a plentiful article in Harrisburg of that day, and what few were here had been having a strenuous time all through the Camp Curtin era and generally found plenty of work without invading the East State street vicinage. Scarce as they were, however, William at length found one. He began to unfold his tale of woe, but he did so most incoherently. The policeman told him to pass on into the night and keep quiet. But William was insistent, so that man with a club and a badge ran him in.

The next day William had gathered unto himself increased incoherency as he meditated upon his wrongs. But Major Augustus L. Roumfort kindly told him that as the walking was fairly good and the "Camelback" still spanning the Susquehanna, he might use it to travel Adams county way, providing he used it inside of fifteen minutes.

Today (unless he has died very recently), William is a prosperous retired old farmer of Kansas, with an ample store of this world's goods. He made it by ignoring the seductive pasteboards and going down to forty years of hard labor in a new land.

Yet, ever and anon, as he lights his corncob pipe and strokes the hayseed out of his white whiskers, a little of the old Adam surges into him; and he tells the younkers of the present generation what a mighty man he was in his time at "old sledge" and "draw poker."

But, should anyone happen to ask him if he ever tried any of the gambling dens of East State street, Harrisburg, the utterances of his lips would be unfit to print. One sentence of them would turn the reputation of this entire series.

William's case was no isolated one. He simply fared as did hundreds of others, during the Civil war and for long years thereafter, who tempted fate and took their lives in their hands by going into a gambling den of the "Old Eighth Ward."

There traveling men, intent on seeing the sights, lost their cash and became defaulters. These business men, in more than one case, laid the foundation of financial ruin and bankruptcy. These young men squandered the money abstracted from their employers and laid the foundation for long years of bitter remorse.

Did the Eighth Ward notorieties that battened on the losses and sorrows of others—the high flyers of the so-called sporting fraternity of forty or fifty years ago, profit thereby?

I will answer that in the next number of this series.

Walnut Street was the southern boundary of the portion of the Eighth Ward to be razed. This view looks east up Walnut Street from Fourth Street. (HSDC)

17. The Ultimate of the Eighth Ward Gambling Fraternity

March 10, 1913

Through the assiduous work of the officials in charge of purchasing and demolishing the properties needed for the Capitol Park extension, the "Old Eighth" is beginning to put on a very ragged look. As one watches the destruction of some of the frame buildings which have stood for fifty years or more, the visitor to the district is given a graphic view of how flimsy and unsubstantial they were. Especially is this the case where several of them were erected in a row, with no dividing wall, so that the abutting house to the one torn down is left in sorry plight.

I have watched the destruction of some of these shacks, that at some time in their long career, have been speakeasies, gambling halls, and foul dens of prostitution. Around some linger legends of deeds of bestiality and depravity that seem almost unbelievable. It seems odd that so much sin and crime could be condensed within a space so limited as the cramped rooms of these little time-worn tenements. As I gazed at one in particular, memory called up some of the spectacular gamblers, who once flourished in the "Eighth," and who pulled off many a game similar to those played on William, the soldier whose misfortunes have appeared in recent numbers of this series.

The old time gambler, as found in the Eighth Ward in Civil War days and for many years after, was a loud dresser. He affected clothing with broad, pronounced bars; and he especially delighted in jewelry, some of which was genuine and valuable, but oftener of the flashy and paste order.

Misery of a Gambler's Life

These olden-time Eighth Ward gamblers would have told you they were jolly, care-free sports, just as all gamblers the world over, then as now, will claim that theirs is a happy life. And often unsuspecting youth were imposed on by the hideous falsehood and aimed to reach the same life as the acme of earthly bliss. In all the ranks of humanity there is no class more completely sundered from all knowledge of true happiness than the gambler, with one solitary exception, and that exception is a class that was plentifully represented also in the "Old Eighth" and will be considered in a later part of this series. To the inveterate gambler joy is a will-o'-the-wisp, the world of the present to him is as hollow as his own laugh, and the future is as rayless of hope as the sable of a funeral pall. This has been illustrated, again and again, in the lives and in the sorrowful tragic deaths of the men who once plied their profession in the "Eighth."

WHERE THEY CAME FROM

Harrisburg produced a fair crop of gamblers of its own—men to the manor born and bred, or who had located here at so early a period in life as to be recognized as of Ward dens. As one crop died off, another came on to tread the same evil path the end of which is always enveloped with clouds without a silver lining. Some of these men stuck persistently to the "Eighth," some roamed far and wide. It was all one in the end. All made money—made it dishonestly; and that money was as evanescent and deceptive as the mirage in the desert. Most of them died tragically. The few who reached advanced years lived in squalid poverty dependent on charity.

This is a view of the corner of Walnut Street and Tanner's Alley. (HSDC)

In September 1849, black citizens gathered on Short Street to protect runaway slaves from southern slave catchers. (HSDC)

Amongst the recruits to the gambling fraternity, whose special ground was the "Eighth," who came rushing into our town at various periods, some half century ago, because they had heard that here was an alluring field, were some of almost national reputation in their particular line. The military barracks had long made Carlisle a brisk and sporty town in more than one evil pursuit; and, from Carlisle, Charley Foulk and "Bully" Fields drifted into the "Eighth" Ward semi-occasionally to add to the gaiety of places that had plenty doing all hours of the day and night during the Civil war and for at least twenty years thereafter.

Other experts with the pasteboards as all-round gamblers, or who confined themselves to the three card monte trick, who made the Eighth Ward their headquarters for longer or shorter times were "Doc" Greene, "Three-fingered Jack," "Country Ned," a man of magnificent appearance standing fully six feet, two inches, and an immaculate dresser, "English" Charley, George Haight, also a man of fine presence, George Mason, and "Yankee" Bill, a product of the tow-path, who first started Harrisburg life as a bouncer and general utility man in a low dive and gradually rose to the proprietorship.

Of the few prominent outsiders mentioned above who operated in the "Old Eighth," for a greater or less period, in the olden time, one died very suddenly at Hot Springs, Ark., because the other man was a trifle quicker with the trigger; another was burned up in his shack in the Leadville mining region; a third, when last heard from was doing twenty years in Joliet penitentiary; a fourth committed suicide at Memphis when the fickle goddess of chance had stripped him of his last penny.

HOW ONE BUNCH LEFT WASHINGTON

The olden time Eighth Ward gambler roamed far and wide when business grew dull at home, and they heard of places where the pickings were fat and suckers were plenty.

The Grand Review of 1865 had been held and the veterans, crowded around Washington, were being forwarded to their Northern homes. This was a glow of operation. The single railroad between Washington and Baltimore could not handle great masses very expeditiously.

The train on which I was, had been some four hours in getting half a mile from its starting place. It was about leaving a switch for the fifth time, with a fair chance of having the right of way at last, when across the meadows east of the Capitol, four men came running toward the slowly moving cars at a great pace. It was the early dawn and, after a short stern chase, the quartet managed to board the car I was on and took a seat near me. I recognized three of the four as men who had made quite a reputation, in the Eighth Ward, as all-round gamblers in Camp Curtin days. One was a life long resident of the Ward, whom I will call Noah because that is not the least bit like his true handle. The other two drifted away from the town about 1869, and, probably, drifted to perdition for aught I know to the contrary.

I soon noticed that Noah was the magnet of attraction. The other three fairly surrounded him on all sides. They clung to him more closely than the Siamese twins to each other. If Noah had occasion to go to another part of the car, all three were with him. I never saw more tender solicitude for anyone than those men had for Noah.

Presently one of the men suggested to Noah that it would be the proper thing for them to have another ocular demonstration that everything was safe, and he pulled, from a capacious inner pocket, about the largest wad of money I had ever seen. There were twenties and fifties and hundreds all huddled together, with some notes of lower denominations. Noah, years after, told me the roll contained $8,000 and it doubtless did.

There had been a little game in Washington the night before, and the Harrisburg party, deeming fresh air and a quick change of scenery desirable, had not taken time to divide, so from force of circumstances, Noah was the treasurer till Baltimore could be reached.

The party left the train at the first suburban stop in Baltimore. As they filed down a sparsely built mud street, a man on either side had Noah by the arm, whilst the third was tagged on to his coat tail.

This was not Noah's only fat pull. He made many a rich one in Harrisburg from fools that drifted into his Eighth Ward den. Yet he died in penury supported by charity.

18. The State Street Bridge Gang

March 17, 1913

From 1873 on, for a period of twenty years, nothing gave the Old Eighth Ward a more malodorous record than the State street bridge gang.

With the growth of Harrisburg east of the P.R.R. tracks and the multiplication of those tracks, travel between the two sections of the city became an ever growing problem. Deaths and serious accidents, at the numerous crossings, were constantly increasing. East State was a main thoroughfare and outlet of travel for the town. It was the most direct route for reaching Harrisburg's only cemetery of that period. With the opening of the State Street Market, it became an imperative necessity to devise some means by which farmers could reach it, so the State street bridge became Harrisburg's first serious effort to afford some safety to teams and pedestrians crossing the railroad.

It was completed in 1873. The citizens of Harrisburg of that decade were very proud of it. It was one step toward safety, and, possibly, in its youth, it may have been a thing of beauty. At all events citizens whose route of travel lay over the railroad at the risk of life and limb, were not disposed to be critical, on the same principle that we are cautioned not to examine too cautiously the age marks on the molars of a gift horse.

As to this bridge, I opine that its age of loveliness, if it ever had one, has vanished. Yet by repairing it, time and again, to keep it from tumbling on the tracks below, it still serves the needs of foot passenger, dray, cart and farm wagon, as well as the whizzing trolley car. Traffic's procession over it is brisk and incessant.

How Bridge Gang Was Born

The Eighth Ward, at that time, had plenty of toughs. Conditions were there to foster their existence. Houses of infamy of a low type were plentiful on East State, Canal, Spruce, Cowden, and several abutting streets. Saloons were plentiful in the same section, and they were of no exalted character. But heretofore the toughs had lacked a common rallying point. Now, by general consent, they adopted the new bridge as their rendezvous.

On the right corner of the intersection of State and Fifth Street, looking north to North Street, is the Miller Bakery. On the left corner is the H.G. Walter Meat Market. (HSDC)

Gangs which terrorized peaceable citizens, at night and often in the day, were not unknown to Harrisburg of that period. They adopted such names as "the Sixteen Bleeders" and other euphonious and suggestive appellations. But "the Bridge Gang" soon eclipsed them all in an evil record. The bad reputation of the gang was not undeserved. It became a terror to those whose pursuits took them in this section, day or night, but especially at the latter period.

Around the State street bridge the members of the gang held high carnival; and riotings, fights, robberies, and a miscellaneous line of debaucheries were the concomitants of their orgies.

A STATE STREET MURDER

Only a year after the bridge was built an inoffensive young man was murdered on East State street in broad daylight—brutally done to death. He attempted to seek shelter in a business place from the cruel shower of stones rained on him by his cowardly assailants, and was ruthlessly thrust forth and the door barred on him, because the proprietor feared the vengeance of the gang.

The whole affair was seen by numerous citizens; the perpetrators of the crime were well known; there were Eighth Ward officers of the law who were cognizant of their names, yet they escaped unscathed of justice.

Waterloo for the "Bridge Gang"

Soon after, however, the emboldened gang tackled the wrong man. He was of medium size, compactly built, some forty years of age, an ex-officer of the U.S. Regulars, and very handy with his fists, a stranger in the city, who had wandered bridgeway. A stout ruffian of the gang suddenly seized him. Another commenced going through his clothes, whilst a half dozen other hoodlums crowded around.

Then, in less than a pair of seconds, things happened. The pocket-examiner was knocked into a somersault that brought his head violently on the iron railroad tracks, and the subsequent proceedings interested him no more. Wrenching himself loose, the victim-to-be planted right, left where it would do most good for the man in whose grasp he had been pinioned. One of the gang drew a murderous blade. But he never used it. It was two weeks before he took the bandages off his optics.

Your brutal tough is always a coward. The way the heroes of that "bridge gang" tumbled over each other to escape the tornado let loose on them was a caution. Some jumped pell-mell into the canal. Some made time up the tracks roundhouse way, as if sprinting for a purse. For a year after those worthies were afraid to tackle a six-year-old kid, lest they might inadvertently develop another cyclone.

Sentence Broke Heart of Gang

Then just as the gang was getting its second breath, something else happened. One of the most stalwart rounders held up a man and got the price of a glass of rum. Judge Pearson called it highway robbery and donated him two years in "Cherry Hill." This broke the heart and spirit of the gang and gave its most hardened members a long pause for reflection.

"What! Two years for one measly dime. At that rate it pays better and is a sight less risky to go to work."

And go to work some of them did. The State street bridge is still fairly hale, although somewhat warped with the decrepitude of old age; but the State street "bridge gang" has long been only a memory.

Some of its membership are dead; and, it is more pleasant to add, that some of the younger ones, assisted by the wise counsels of devoted men right in our own city who went into highways and byways to gather them into churches and missions, Sunday schools, and Bible classes—are today, industrious, honest, honorable citizens of this and other communities.

The outline of the State street "bridge gang" and malefactors in other [line missing] . . . one, for it is not a pleasant subject on which to dwell at length. It was a natural product of civic conditions which should never have been permitted to take root to batten on the public and sap the city's vitality. It was the result of disorderly houses that were allowed to flaunt vice in public view and of the unlimited licensing of saloons of a low type. Combined with these causes there was also a measure of political depravity, for the members of the gang had votes and a pull and were unfit to administer. The whole bargain-and-sale political methods in evidence, year after year, in Eighth Ward elections gave an immunity, not only to bawdy houses and speak-easies, but also to the "bridge gang and malefactors in other lines."

A gang as openly defiant as was this one, would last in the Harrisburg of today, a scant twenty-four hours 'ere its members were in jail or else making record time in their search for "the tall timber." After all, those "good old times" we sometimes hear extolled so lavishly, were not always as rosy in reality as exuberant fancy has sometimes painted them.

Near the bridge on State Street, looking back toward the capitol, boys play baseball in the shadows. The State Street Bridge Gang accosted victims here. (HSDC)

19. Industrial Plants, Past and Present: The Bay Foundry

March 24, 1913

At a very early period of its history the district under consideration in this series was the seat of some of the prominent industries of the town. Some of these were located here whilst the population was but sparse, and long before the section had been erected into a separate Ward the oldest industries of the district far antedated those places of infamy, which for several decades gave the Ward an evil name. Some of the earlier plants were located here for convenient access to canal and railroad transportation.

It is the intention of the writer to give some account in this series of every prominent industry which has flourished in the Eighth Ward ere it disappears to be replaced by a beautiful park, although all may not be given consecutively.

The industries and activities under the supervision of his brothers who were long prominent business factors in our city will furnish the material for today's article. Modes in all lines of business have been completely revolutionized in the past half century. Under olden time methods the local foundry was an essential of every community. Harrisburg had several. One of the earliest and most prominent of these was the Bay foundry, established by James Bay, an uncle of William F. Bay and James G.M. Bay. The elder Bay is recalled by some of our older citizens as a rather small man, always very neat in appearance, well dressed, and possessed of fine features.

The first location was on Fourth street directly opposite the present Bethel church, extending half way up to Walnut. Mr. Bay took a partner into the business, the firm name became Bay & Small.

During the winter of 1847-8, the foundry was removed to State street at the intersection of Canal street, which was a busy thoroughfare of the town for many years, until entirely obliterated by the encroachments of railroad tracks. The junior partner owned a lumber yard and saw mill at Wrightsville. Here the timbers for the new foundry were fashioned, being then shipped to this point by canal. It was all picked white pine lumber, well cured, and when the brick work which

The Hickok plant occupied ground where the Bay Foundry once stood. (PSA)

covers it is removed, at the demolition of the building, I would not be surprised if it is found to be in perfect condition. The frame work of the new foundry was erected by Richard Updegrove, a boss carpenter in the town of that day, who was subsequently an alderman in one of the Wards.

Prior to 1852 Mr. Small withdrew from the firm. Subsequently the foundry was rented for a time by John J. Osler, as a teacher in the old Lancasterian building. Of the nephews of James Bay, the founder of the plant, William F. had come to Harrisburg in 1847, and his brother, James G.M., in 1852. About 1863 the brothers formed a partnership as the successors of the uncle.

MAKING CAPITOL PARK IRON FENCE

Many readers will remember the massive iron fence which, at one time, enclosed the Capitol grounds, for it was only during Governor Beaver's administration that it was removed and used to enclose the land around the arsenal. Most of this fence was made at the Bay foundry. What was not made there was constructed at the Jennings foundry which will be the subject of a subsequent article. The iron fencing was not all erected at one time, there having been at least three contracts with the several foundries furnishing it, before the work was completed. The first part of the fence to be built was that along Third street.

In the good old days, when cattle and hogs (the four-legged kind) roamed the streets, fences were considered around all public grounds. The original fence on

The Harrisburg Steam Heat and Power Company had its offices on Short Street, between South Street and Cranberry Alley. The tip of the capitol dome is just visible behind the plant. (PSA)

the Third street side of the Capitol Park was made of posts and rails, the latter being sawed pine about six inches in width. From Pine street a brick wall surmounted by pickets (a favorite mode of fencing in the early days) ran across the grounds from Third street to what is now Fourth street, leaving the lower part of the grounds, which was the original John Harris donation, entirely unfenced. In the fine picture of the Harrisburg of 1855 hanging in the common council chamber in the court house, this brick wall can be distinctly seen.

Great was the enthusiasm of all the citizens when brick wall and post and rail disappeared to be replaced by an iron barricade strong enough to keep out, not cattle only, but herds of the rhinoceros or the elephant. They stood on the corners shaking each other enthusiastically by the hands; and it was then that was born the talismanic cry: "Watch Harrisburg grow."

Some years later, when councils passed a belated ordinance forbidding the roaming on the streets of cattle, swine, sheep and the like, Harrisburg was not quite so proud of its iron barrier. First the iron gates were torn away, and later the authorities decreed the passing of the fence. About the same time another Capitol Park landmark disappeared. The board walk from the building to Third and Walnut street, which in various gradations of dilapidation, had done duty for a generation, was replaced by a granolithic walk.

A Picturesque Olden Time Character

A familiar figure at the Bay foundry plant, both on Fourth street and for many years after the removal to State street, was a gigantic negro of herculean strength, Aaron Bennett by name, a brother of the "king" Bennett mentioned in a former article of this series. At first a cupola tender, he was afterwards employed to assist in molding, and was a trusty all round hand of the elder Bay and of the brothers who succeeded him. He was a quiet, industrious man, whose boast in his prime was that he could drink two quarts of whisky a day without showing any effect therefrom.

When the Bay Bros. retired about 1883, a number of lessees followed. The brick walls of the desolate building still bear the legends of some of them. On the railroad front appears in time-worn letters: "Harvie & Bickley, founders and machinists." On the State street side: "John W. Brown, foundry and machine Works."

The first lessee was the firm of Brown & Reed composed of John W. Brown and Augustus Reed. At the same time the retired Bay Bros., in a small adjoining building of the same property, were conducting a real estate agency. Under Brown & Reed the plant was known as the "Phoenix Works." It was also sometimes styled the "Harrisburg foundry." After Mr. Reed withdrew from the firm, Mr. Brown conducted the business for some years by himself; but, in 1894, I find that it was run as John W. Brown & Co., the partner being Mercer B. Tate.

This photograph shows a close-up view of the Steam Heat and Power Company's entrance. (HSDC)

After Mr. Brown finally retired from the iron business and gave his declining days to forwarding the work of the Lafayette Rescue Mission, the next lessees of the plant were Harvie & Bickley, the partners being J.C. Harvie and W.H.H. Bickley. The last occupant of the foundry in 1905 was the Harrisburg Iron Co., J.P. Luce, manager. This business was short-lived, since which time the once busy foundry has stood in desolation, evincing many marks of age. In the meantime the Bay Bros., up to the time of the death of William F., in 1899, and James G.M. since that time, have been prominent factors in the city's activities. They were connected with the "Penna. Ammonia and Fertilizer Co.," "the Harrisburg Steam Stone Works" and other industries. Their best remembered enterprise was the erection and operation of the Bay Shoe factory located on the same plot as the foundry. This will be spoken of briefly in the next article of this series.

The south side of the Steam Heat and Power Company shows more of its considerable size and rather shabby appearance. (PSA)

20. INDUSTRIAL PLANTS, PAST AND PRESENT: THE BAY SHOE CO., W.O. HICKOK MANUFACTURING CO., DAUPHIN CIGAR CO.

MARCH 31, 1913

Although the Bay Shoe Co. was a comparatively recent addition to the industrial enterprises of the Eighth Ward, not having been formed until after the Bay Bros. had ceased active work at the foundry, yet substantially one fourth of a century has passed since the erection at State and Poplar streets of the immense factory building in which it was housed. It was a three story brick of modern construction with a frontage of some forty feet on State street and extending back to North alley a distance of almost 240 feet. Begun in 1887, it was enlarged the following year. The original officers of the company were president, William F. Bay; treasurer, James G.M. Bay. Upon the death of William F. Bay in 1899, his brother James became president. For a term of years the factory did an extensive business in the shoe manufacturing, employing several hundred workmen and sending its products to many points in the United States and Canada.

Following the burning of the Main Capitol building and the demolition of the office building flanking it, to make way for the erection of the New Capitol, the State was compelled to house the various governmental departments in rented properties. Most of them were accommodated in the Bay building which was leased by the State for a period of four years. During this time Mr. James Bay had his office in a small building adjoining the foundry, active work in the factory having been discontinued.

About five years since, the W.O. Hickok Manufacturing Company purchased all of the Bay plot and added it to their already extensive holdings. With the change of ownership the factory building was utilized in housing the Dauphin Cigar Co., an important industry established in 1903, which was located originally in a large frame building of the Hickok plant facing the P.R.R. The cigar company

The E.N. Cooper Foundry was next to the Steam Heat and Power Company. The roof of the Wesley Union A.M.E. Zion Church and the capitol dome can be seen in the background. (PSA)

was successful from the first and has a large number of employees, principally female. The Superintendent is F.C. Seegers. His predecessor was C.E. McCurdy.

W.O. HICKOK MANUFACTURING CO.

The most extensive industrial plant in the Capitol park extension district is that of the W.O. Hickok Manufacturing Co., known as the "Eagle Works." It is also the oldest prominent industry established in that section, and the only one of the original industries that has come down to the present time with no radical changes in ownership or location. From a rather humble beginning, more than three-fourths of a century ago, it has seen a steady growth that has attained colossal proportions.

The founder, W.O. Hickok, a man of only medium stature but of great physical activity, was a prominent man of his day who did much for the development of the infant activities of Harrisburg. In him urbanity, positiveness and prompt decision were mingled in such proportions as to make him popular with those associated with him. He took a great interest in the borough of Harrisburg, was chosen by its citizens as one of their councilmen and served as president of that body. Here he was associated with such men as General Simon Cameron, William Calder, John Briggs, John Berryhill, Al Hamilton and others equally illustrious in the history of the town, for, at that time, it was a Harrisburg custom to select the foremost citizens as members of council.

The "Eagle Works" were at first located on Strawberry street east of Third in very diminutive quarters, but, in a few years, the excellence of the work done had created so great a demand for the machinery turned out that it became necessary to seek a location where there was room for expansion. Accordingly, in 1844, removal was made to the present site and buildings erected at North and Canal streets. New buildings have been constructed, from time to time, as business needs demanded them, until now they number about fourteen of various kinds. These are spread over a plot which has been enlarged by additions until it comprises almost two acres.

The works were greatly enlarged in 1869. In 1886 from being the individual property of Mr. Hickok, the sphere of activities of the "Eagle Works" was extended by the incorporation of the W.O. Hickok Manufacturing Co. In 1890 extensive new works were erected, in 1907, as already stated, the contiguous Bay plant was purchased, and soon after the mammoth wooden building facing the P.R.R., which had been a landmark of that portion of the city since 1860, was demolished, its days of usefulness having passed.

During all the years of this development the motto adopted by Mr. Hickok when he started his little plant on Strawberry street—"Finis Coronat Opus"—has been the guiding star of the management. The officials of the company have been prompt at all times, to avail themselves of all advantages afforded by the advances of invention and science. The "Eagle Works" were amongst the first industrial plants of the land to employ electricity exclusively both as a light and for motive power.

VARIED MANUFACTURES

First and last the "Eagle Works" have manufactured more than one hundred lines of complicated machinery, including feed cutters, cider mills, all kinds of machine castings, the many varieties of mechanics' tools, paper ruling machines, paper ruling pens, bookbinders' machinery, printers' machinery, school furniture, as well as all forms of general machine work. Not only has the W.O. Hickok Mfg. Co. acquired celebrity throughout the United States for superior excellence in bookbinding and printing machinery, but Harrisburg work is honored in foreign lands in the fact that at the present time, thirteen foreign governments have adopted the bookbinding machinery made by the Hickok company for use in their respective government printing offices. On an average, one-third of the output of the plant bounded by North, State and Poplar streets and the P.R.R. goes to foreign lands, the distribution reaching every portion of the civilized world.

The various leading products of the works, at different times, afford a striking commentary on vast changes in various economic conditions which have occurred in three-fourths of a century. Early in the history of W.O. Hickok's work his principal line was feed cutters and cider mills. Indeed it was with these two articles that he scored his initial success and extended the fame of the "Eagle Works" through all the rural portions of the United States. At a later period, when

At the eastern border of the Eighth was the W.O. Hickok Manufacturing Company, maker of a wide range of machines, especially school furniture, bicycles, and bookbinding machinery. (HSDC)

common School development had begun to take advanced ground, school furniture was the leading output. With the development of modern building methods, sash weight and cellar grates became prominent amongst the products of the Hickok plant. A decade and a half ago, when the bicycle fad was at its height, this company took high rank amongst the manufacturers of that article.

The principal departments of the works today are brass and iron foundries; a department for all kinds of general repair work; another for automobile repairing; departments for wood working, painting, polishing and planing; and the gear cutting room. The company has a location secured to which it will remove whenever the State takes over the present site.

OFFICIALS OF HICKOK COMPANY

Mr. W.O. Hickok, founder of the "Eagle" plant and first president of the company, died in 1893. He was followed in the presidency by Robert Snodgrass for a number of years. Then for twelve years, Christian W. Lynch was at the helm. The present head of the company is W.O. Hickok, 3rd. Associated with him in the management are F.J. Brady, treasurer, and Ross A. Hickok, secretary. A prominent official of the past was L.S. Bigelow, for several years general manager and secretary.

Samuel Schriver, of 434 Boas street, very recently retired, was associated with the "Eagle Works" for fifty-seven years, during about one-half of which time he was the treasurer of the company. Indeed, the number of employees who have been at these one works for a lifetime stands out as a very prominent eulogium upon the management of the Hickok company when contrasted with the constant changes and ceaseless labor agitations of the present day. There are quite a number of workmen there today who have been in the employ of the company forty years or more, and a large number who have worked in these shops for over thirty years.

One of the most conspicuous examples of long service was the case of Albert Cooper, who died in February, 1909, after an active career of fifty-seven years at the "Eagle Works." He invented or perfected many of the things manufactured by the company. Perhaps the most important of these was the ruling machine now in use the wide world over from New York to the Philippines, in India and Australia and from Alaska to the extremities of South America. For some of his inventions he received awards of honor from the Columbian Exposition of 1893 at Chicago.

This Hickok advertisement in the 1902 Harrisburg Telegraph *gives the impression of an imperial, industrial complex. State government operated out of here temporarily after the old capitol burned down at the turn of the century.*

21. Industrial Plants, Past and Present: The Paxton Flour and Feed Co., The Harrisburg Storage Co., The Benitz Corner, The Roger Sheehy Corner

April 7, 1913

One of the most extensive business plants of the district is located on the plot containing the building of the Paxton Flour and Feed Co., and the Harrisburg Storage Co., both under the same management. This plot comprises substantially the square enclosed by State, Poplar and South streets and the P.R.R. Title has already passed to the State, the consideration being $96,500.

The Paxton Flour and Feed Company was organized in 1872, the partners being John Hoffer, Levi Brandt and the James McCormick estate. About fourteen years later Mr. Hoffer dropped out of the firm. The business was continued by the remaining members of the firm for nineteen years until, by the death of Levi Brandt, his interests in the business passed to his sons, D. Bailey Brandt and J. Austin Brandt.

Thus the business has been carried on for forty continuous years in the same location without any radical change in ownership.

During all this time the plant which is directly alongside of the P.R.R., with its own siding, has been recognized as one of the leading grain shipping centers of Central Pennsylvania. The company handles grain for farmers and are jobbers of flour to grocers, bakers, and the trade generally. It also handles every species of feeds and field seeds. The Harrisburg grain elevator of the firm has a capacity of unloading twelve cars per day and can hoist 2,500 bushels per hour.

But the activities of the company are not confined to its Harrisburg headquarters. It owns nine other grain elevators at various points of the Cumberland Valley, the entire bin capacity of the company's elevators being

175,000 bushels. From these points wheat, oats and other grains are shipped to the New England States and various other points.

For many years the company did an extensive business in canal shipments, until, with a folly that many are now regretting, the canals of our State, by a sort of general acquiescence, were allowed to lapse into oblivion.

THE HARRISBURG STORAGE CO.

The Harrisburg Storage Company, incorporated, was organized ten years ago. The interests represented in the Company are the James McCormick estate and the brothers, D. Bailey and J. Austin Brandt. The six-story fireproof warehouse of the company is one of the most complete and up-to-date buildings in Harrisburg, with a storage capacity of two hundred cars. The substantial nature of the structure can be inferred from the fact that its floors have a thickness of six inches, whilst the upright timbers of the building have faces of sixteen by sixteen inches. No mortar was used in the construction, all the brick being laid with cement.

THE BENITZ CORNER

After delaying, through several numbers of this series, around the old State street bridge with accounts of industrial plants and of other things that were far from

The view north toward State Street railroad bridge from the east end of the Eighth. (HSDC)

being industrial, I will, for a short time, write of a busy business corner in an entirely different part of the Park extension. It has been known for years as the Benitz corner, and is located at the corner of Walnut and Short streets.

This section is now so compactly built that yards are an unknown luxury, yet, within the memory of citizens yet living, it was a productive truck patch farmed by honest old John Osler who resided on Walnut street opposite the opening of Tanner. The oldest buildings in this section were the Young residence and butcher shop at 506 and 508 Walnut street. All else up to the corner of Short street was the Osler truck patch. John Osler had a number of sons, who were prominent in the activities of the old burg, one of these being Thomas, the olden time teacher at the Lancasterian school building where now stands the Technical High School. He it was whom, when the Democrats of Harrisburg grew enthusiastic in the Polk campaign of 1844, bestrode an enormous ox on a float in their mammoth street parade, the ox, later in the same day, being roasted in approved style in the Capitol grounds and served to the hungry marchers. Just here, let me remark parenthetically and entirely irrelevantly, that, at present meat prices, the serving up of an ox of the girth of that ox of 1844 would require an Andy Carnegie or a John D. to do the financing.

Not directly connected with our main subject it may be interesting to note in passing that John Osler finally disposed of his Eighth Ward holdings in exchange for five acres of land beginning on North Third street at the present Hemler home No. 918 and extending up to Herr and back to Penn streets. It was not till 1868 that the breaking up of this tract in lots, and building upon some of them began.

THE WORK OF CONSTANTINE BENITZ

In 1848 an intelligent German, John Weiss by name, was so closely identified with the revolution which swept over the Fatherland that year that, when the insurgents were crushed and the monarchy re-established, he deemed it would be conducive to his health to take a vacation in America. He started a saddle and harness making shop at 424-426 Walnut street where Nathan Brenner is now in business. To him, in 1861, came Constantine Benitz, young and industrious. So industrious was he that by 1863, he had not only mastered the trade, but married the proprietor's daughter. In November of the same year he opened a little shop on the corner, which has ever since been identified with his name.

Benitz remained in business till 1889 when he sold the trade. In 1895 a son of Mr. Benitz opened in the corner, remaining there for ten years. His successors have been the Franklin Tea Co., and Meyer Gross, who commenced business on the adjacent corner.

Part of the land on which the buildings of the St. Lawrence congregation were erected was sold to Father Koppernagle by Mr. Benitz, who, at one time, had owned the entire tract to Angle alley. In 1877 he erected the building at 448 Walnut street, adjoining the church, whilst, in 1895, he constructed the substantial row of four residences running from 438 to 444 Walnut street. Previous to the erection of these houses there had been no building between the church edifice and the corner store except an old time carpenter shop.

THE ROGER SHEEHY CORNER

Across Short street from the Benitz corner is a building which has long been identified, in Harrisburg history, with a multiplicity of business which it would be unprofitable to trace in detail even if such a thing were now possible. The corner store room has generally been a grocery.

The building, which has been recently remodeled and improved following a conflagration, was erected by Roger Sheehy eighty years ago, and has come lineally to his descendants to the present time.

Sheehy, an emigrant from Ireland, was an excellent stonemason, and coming to Harrisburg at a time when workmen of his craft were not very numerous, soon had a lucrative business. Prior to the days of street paving a prominent part of the city's work was placing stone crossings at street intersections. A large amount of this work was done by Roger Sheehy.

The Roger Sheehy corner was named for the shop of an Irish stone mason. Benitz corner was across the street. (PSA)

22. Speakeasies of the "Old Eighth"

April 14, 1913

The "Old Eighth" was always well supplied with licensed places for the sale of liquors. Yet was it also fruitful in speakeasies. These unlicensed places were of various grades. At a time when the Ward was filled with houses of prostitution all of these derived a considerable portion of their revenues from the sales of wines and other beverages for which enormous prices were demanded.

There were other speakeasies of the Eighth devoted exclusively to the trade in intoxicants which was especially brisk on Sundays. There was a time in Harrisburg when well known customers could gain easy access to many barrooms on a Sabbath morning.

But, about 1874, Judge Pearson on the Dauphin county bench became so severe with those that infringed on the liquor laws of the State that landlords generally closed their bars very tightly on that day.

Then along Tanner, Cranberry and South streets, and some of the narrow courts which led from them arose a multitude of speakeasies to supplement those which already existed on State, Spruce and Filbert streets and at other spots east of the Capitol. Each Sunday morning crowds of eager-eyed men might be seen pouring out North street and across the Capitol grounds toward these resorts.

There was little style about the Eighth Ward speakeasy and the stuff sold in them was generally the cheapest and vilest that could be purchased. Some of the proprietors conducted the business so persistently, with little molestation from the authorities, that they acquired a neat sum of money in that way.

Recently I watched the demolition of a house on old Spruce street long inhabited by a very king in the illegal liquor sale business. As keen customers would come to his door of a Sunday, he would assume a show of righteous wrath, shouting out, "What do you mean by coming thumping at my door? Don't you know it is the holy Sabbath day?" Then he would quickly add in an audible whisper, "Go in at the gate."

And in at the gate they went by ones, twos and threes, till his house was filled to overflowing. All comers were welcome, minors, habitual drunkards, or what not,—only so they had the prices.

Bertha Lewis Went on the Rampage in the Eighth Ward and Lands in Jail.

Bertha Lewis, an Eighth ward colored damsel, who is charged with being of a very jealous disposition is in jail on numerous criminal charges, all of which are felonious assault and battery with attempt to kill, two being preferred yesterday by Thomas Mosley and Etta Green. This latter offense was committed late yesterday afternoon on Cowden street near State, and nearly caused a riot. As a result of the shooting one of Bertha's victims was obliged to go to the hospital for treatment for a bullet wound in his right thigh.

This story shows the prose style and point of view that were meant to entertain both this reporter's and J. Howard Wert's readers a century ago.

A GOOD LIVING IN IT

I watched the destruction of another house, on a Main street, once occupied by a man who had joined the "Sons of Ease." He adopted illegal liquor selling as a means of livelihood. Once when a friend told him of a job he could obtain, his reply was, "Me want a job? Not on your life. I can take in enough coin on Sunday to pay the rent, do the marketing and buy myself clothes. As to the old woman let her earn her own clothes."

But many of the men who ran speakeasies in dilapidated shacks of the "Old Eighth" tried to augment their profits by combining gambling with the selling of drinks, craps being the most common game. From these was evolved, by degrees, the political speakeasy, run by some petty precinct worker, with a supposed pull, who was shrewd enough to pocket the money given him by the leaders to influence elections, and, at the same time rob the men who frequented his joint by selling them the cheapest and worst grade of booze at the highest figures, and also by raking in their hard-earned wages at the gaming table.

Sometimes the speakeasy of this class cloaked itself under some high sounding club appellation, each victim paying a dime or a quarter for a key, and thus constituting himself a member of the club. The *Patriot*, at various times, was a

NO. 428 HURT.

No. 428, who is an Austrian working for Drake & Stratton on the railroad improvements near Duncannon, was hurt this morning by a falling rail. Some laborers were unloading rails from a truck and one of the rails slipping from the truck fell on the left leg of No. 428 and badly sprained it. He was taken to the city hospital, where he said he was married and had several children in Austria. His name, however, was too much for the attendants at the hospital and none of them undertook to write it down. No. 428 was hardly strong enough to say it all at once himself.

This kind of story suggests the difference between "the good old days" and present times. In this instance, the Telegraph *of 1902 has some fun with an unfortunate immigrant.*

prominent factor in exposing some of the speakeasies run on this principle and in putting them out of business.

INSIDE SCENES

It was, perhaps, some twenty-five years ago that a guileless Harrisburger, desiring to see life from its different angles, visited a speakeasy of the "Old Eighth" under the guiding care of a jolly fellow around town who had once been on the police force and who was supposed to know the ropes. The guide I will call Billy Jelly because the name has a euphonious sound. The experience obtained on the visit of investigation, as narrated afterwards by the one in search of knowledge, are here given in a much condensed form.

The building was a sickly looking frame structure on a narrow alley. After a peculiar rap on the front door, it was cautiously opened a short distance. Billy Jelly muttered something to the guardian which procured admission for him and his companion. Immediately after was heard the hard, rasping sound of a bolt being forced into place.

After advancing through two small vacant rooms, a stairway leading to the second floor was reached. Near the foot of this, seated on an upturned box, was a heavy-set man of most unprepossessing features. On either side of him was a box similar to the one on which he was seated, on one of which stood a demijohn, whilst the other was the resting place for a keg on its side the spigot of which protruded over the edge of the box. A half dozen glasses of different sizes completed the furnishings.

"Here's where we do the libation act," muttered Billy Jelly to his companion. "They would spot anyone that cut out the booze. I'll try to pick the less pisenous."

"A couple of the hard stuff, you bunch of beauty," continued Billy Jelly aloud. Hereupon the seated figure deliberately raised a flap door in the soap box on which stood the demijohn and drew forth a black bottle from which he filled two very diminutive glasses.

The Harrisburg explorer had hardly downed his drink until he experienced a strange feeling of strangulation suggestive of a stream of lava coursing inside of him.

"Keep a stiff upper lip," whispered Billy Jelly encouragingly; "the worst will soon be over."

"What was that awful stuff? Was it poison?" gasped the searcher after life as seen in the "Old Eighth."

"Some men have survived several doses," was Jelly's equivocal reply.

"But what was it?"

"Some humorists," replied Jelly, "call it whiskey. It is a brand only found in its purity and full flavor in an Eighth Ward crap joint or political club just previous to an election. It's a leetle tough on the carcass but I selected it in preference to the slops. If you had taken a schooner of the stuff in the gek, manufactured especially for the "Hunky" trade, there would have been a homesick and unquiet feeling in your department of internal affairs for some days to come. They economize on the hard stuff and give very small doses. Therein lies the protection of the victim."

"Come Seven! Come Eleven!" were the cries which greeted the pair of explorers as they reached the second floor. A crap game was in full swing and the perspiring and gesticulating players were most enthusiastic. It was a motley crowd that was present and the little room was reeking with foul odors. The visitor piloted by Billy Jelly managed to get off in a corner where, unseen by the excited players, he secured a little fresh air by breaking the crown paper pasted over a missing window pane.

To add to the miseries of the situation some one raised the alarm (whether true or false the visitor never knew) that the police were in the offing and that no one should be admitted or permitted to leave till the ban was lifted. Thus marooned, the searcher after Eighth Ward knowledge spent weary hours as he vowed never again to permit inquisitiveness to walk away with judgment.

23. The National Hotel. Some Other Hotels, Past and Present, of the "Old Eighth"

April 21, 1913

Reader of this series, have you ever paused to consider the magnitude of the razing operations now being conducted by the State of Pennsylvania in the Old Eighth Ward? Of course there has been more extended work of the same character in the very large cities of Europe and, to some extent, in those of the United States.

Recently it was announced that the French government was confronted with a serious problem of finding accommodations for 120,000 homeless persons who were to be evicted from their dwellings, owing to the conversion of the twelve-mile circle of antiquated Parisian fortifications into park land. What had been, in olden time, the 500 yards space of the firing zone in front of these works, had been gradually built up with ramshackle houses inhabited largely by rag pickers and criminals. Now, the fortifications, which were built in 1840 at an expense of $200,000,000, and the thousands of tenements of the firing zone are doomed alike to be leveled.

It is doubtful, however, if in this new world there has ever been a demolition of buildings in a city no larger than Harrisburg, carried forward on a larger scale than the present operations in the Eighth Ward. Whilst a large number of these structures are antiquated, yet there are a number of massive ones of modern construction. One of these affords the material for the opening section of this number.

The National Hotel

The fine location at Fourth and State streets, where now stands the National Hotel and the State Street Market House, remained a vacant lot after the greater part of East State street, between the Capitol grounds and the P.R.R., had been

The National Hotel is on the corner in this turn-of-the-century photograph of the intersection of State and North Fourth Streets. (HSDC)

pretty completely built. About 1870 a company of enterprising citizens started to improve it by the erection of a hotel building and a structure for a market.

The hotel at first only occupied a portion of the building, fronting on State street. The rooms in the corner at Fourth and State were applied, for some years, to a variety of uses, amongst which were a tinner's shop, a grocery store and a drug store. Then James Costello transformed them into a pool room and cigar store. When the building was remodeled in 1893, these rooms became a portion of the enlarged hotel.

The first landlord in the new hotel was a Mr. Fishburn, who kept it in 1871 and 1872. He was followed, in 1873, by our well known fellow citizen, the genial Philip McGill, who was in partnership with J.P. Dougherty. Following these for short terms were Samuel Notestine and a landlord named Buck.

CHARLES MCCULLOUGH AT THE NATIONAL

Then there came to the National an enterprising landlord, who soon developed it into a hotel of considerable prominence. This was Chas. McCullough, veteran of the Civil War, who had a host of warm friends in Harrisburg.

In the olden time almost any kind of a shanty along State street could get a license, and indeed there are comparatively few of the buildings along this thoroughfare which have attained an age of fifty years or more which did not, at

101

The Hotel Frye is on the left corner in this photograph of the intersection of State and Fifth Streets, looking south toward the Corona Hotel at Fifth and South Streets. (HSDC)

some time, display a tavern sign. As an illustration, the little building at the northeast corner of Filbert and State streets was at one time a full fledged hotel.

Occasionally the whole equipment of a licensed State street hotel of the long ago was contained in one room of a rented basement, and it was thus that "Charley" McCullough started, as a Harrisburg landlord, in a basement near the Wagner bakery, east of old Spruce street. He then removed to 441 State street, and soon after, located at the corner of State and Spruce which, up to that time, had been Neal's grocery.

This corner long known as the American House, has been a licensed place continuously since it was opened as such by McCullough.

After some years at the American House, McCullough took charge of the National, but, losing his license in 1882, became a landlord on the West side of the Susquehanna and subsequently in Gettysburg.

After being without a license for three years, the National was opened to the public in 1885 by its present landlord, Fred W. Ebel, who has a reputation equally as a courteous hotel keeper, an expert fisherman, and a staunch Democrat. An able aid in maintaining the high standard of the house has been his assistant Horace

(Butch) Benedict. The annexed building to the National, known, for more than 40 years, as the State Street Market, has a history so unique that it is deserving of a full number for itself.

PRESENT HOTELS OF STATE STREET

In addition to the National, five other licensed places now exist along State street, the survivor of a much larger number which have flourished in their day, faded away, and been well nigh forgotten. Of these five, two are on the southern corners of State and Fifth, two on opposite sides of State street at its intersection with Cowden, and one beneath the shadow of the State street bridge quite near the railroad tracks. All of these have been licensed places during a long period of years.

The hotel at the southwest corner of Fifth and State was long conducted by James A. Manger as the American House, he having been the successor of McCullough. Subsequent landlords have been Edmund Foley, who had before kept a saloon at an old stand at the corner of Short and South streets; Amos Warner, Herman Bucher, and Harry T. Smith, who has conducted the place for more than a decade.

THE HISTORIC McCARTHY HOUSE

One of the best known hotel stands of the "Old Eighth" was the one built by Callanghan McCarthy at the northwest corner of State and Cowden streets, where he presided as a genial landlord for more than 40 years. Before establishing himself here, Mr. McCarthy had conducted a saloon on the north side of South street, between Fifth and Cowden. He was a staunch Democrat who, for many years, made himself felt as quite a factor in Eighth Ward politics.

The hotel at 510 State street, corner of Fifth, for many years, had as its landlord the warm-hearted Patrick O'Sullivan. Some of his successors have been F.A. Johnson, Samuel M. McCann, who gave his hostelry the designation XX, and William H. Forbes, at one time Harrisburg's lieutenant of police. The present landlord is Theodore S. Frye, a prominent colored citizen, who is the only one of that race now conducting a hotel in Harrisburg. There have, however, been a number of ventures in that line by colored men, at various periods of the past, some of which present matter so unique that they will receive some notice in a future article.

The licensed place at 523 State street, corner of Cowden, was for many years under the charge of the well known Edward A. Meyer who had a whole host of friends in Harrisburg. After the building was remodeled and improved, about 1904, he bestowed on his hostelry the name LeRoy. Some of Mr. Meyer's successors were A. Sansone and J.N. Weaver.

The old Mitchell stand, at 729 State street, has had a multiplicity of landlords in recent years. It was kept for a time by S.S. Johnston, a former proprietor of the Washington House on Walnut street. Here died the kind-hearted veteran soldier,

William T. Sollers soon after he occupied the place, having been driven from his former hotel on Canal street by the encroachments of the railroad trackage. The hotel was conducted for a time by his widow, Rebecca Sollers, and then successively by J.R. Orner, J.C. Coates, M.A. Heagy, W. Heist, and P.L. Sullivan. It was during Heist's occupancy that a large body of soldiers being conveyed to or from some big event raided the place for eatables and drinkables until it looked as if struck by a cyclone.

A poster-plastered building at 418 Walnut Street shows that live minstrel shows were in competition with the moving picture shows. Fink's Beer was a local brew. (PSA)

24. The State Street Market

April 28, 1913

The last number of this series presented some data about a number of hotels, past and present, of the "Old Eighth." A few more will be given at a subsequent period, especially some around which still hover tales full of human interest. Today, however, I want to talk of the most unique market Harrisburg has ever contained, located in the squat building annexed to the National Hotel.

When the building, which houses the well known State Street Market was erected, it was supposed to fill the proverbial "long felt need." Leading men of the town were back of it with David Mumma at their head. Other prominent citizens of Harrisburg who invested in the enterprise were Mr. Sturgeon, Michael McCloskey, and Daniel Dougherty.

Yet, for years, the market seemed to be a financial failure. At first markets were held on Tuesday and Friday morning and Saturday evening. The morning markets never were well attended either by buyers or sellers, and were soon abandoned. The Saturday evening markets were a success from the first as far as attendance was concerned, and soon became a distinctive show feature of the town.

By 1880 the market company, which had started out with high hopes, had become so badly involved that the property was put up for sale and the entire block of hotel and market buildings become the individual property of Augustus R. Shellenberger.

The first Market master was Charles Swartz, a well-remembered citizen who resided at 2299 [?] State street. He was occasionally assisted by his son, George. After the death of Mr. Swartz, Augustus H. Frankem became market master in 1891, and discharged the onerous duties of the position in a most satisfactory manner until his death, twenty years later.

Saturday Night Scenes

As fell the shades of evening on the last day of each week, the State street market began to fill up until soon it was seething up and overflowing. Here came buyers of course, the hardy sons of toil and their wives who were investing some of the wages just paid in food for the opening days of the week. But for each bona fide patron of the market, there were generally at least a dozen who came for other reasons. Some came out of curiosity, because there was sure to be a motley crowd on hand; some to see and be seen; some from motives that had little of good in them.

In the days when East State street and some of its intersecting thoroughfares were lined with dens of prostitution which were conducted as openly as saloons or grocery stores, the inmates of these places arrayed in gorgeous raiment and often partially intoxicated, came in goodly numbers to the State street market, using every artifice and form of entreaty to allure customers to their haunts.

On more than one occasion two of these women who were desirous of entrapping the same men or who had rankling jealousy of the past to settle, would engage in a hair-pulling and skirt-tearing scrap in the aisles of the market or on the streets of the immediate vicinity.

State Street, Saturday Night

Thirty years ago, when the olden-time State street was still in its prime as an evil resort, the pavements of that street from Fourth street to the railroad tracks was one surging mass of humanity moving hither and thither. Especially was this the case on the southern or market house sides. All the drinking resorts were crowded to the doors and doing a rushing business in the sale of intoxicants. As the beer and whisky mingled with gin, and other brands of disturbance breeders began to get in effective work on the imbibers, there was always plenty doing. Somebody would start something and the instantaneous effect was very like the application of a match to a magazine of gunpowder.

City Editor's Holiday

A former city editor of the *Patriot* now connected with one of the leading journals of the Quaker city, had a quaint way of getting a little recreation when Saturday brought him a night and day of release from his office duties. He would wait around the mayor's office in the Square till the inevitable Saturday night riot call came in from the "Old Eighth," then hop into the patrol car with the officers who were being dispatched to the scene of trouble. A moment more they would all be in the danger zone, between Fourth and Cowden, the brickbats were flying through the atmosphere and razors shining and gleaming in the electric light. No ex-patrolman of Harrisburg but found out that the "Old Eighth" was a strenuous place on a Saturday night.

Some Freak Venders

To the State market came weekly a number of countryside farmers with prime golden butter, tempting fat fowls and other delicacies of the farm. But venders from the city were also largely represented, and some of them brought stuff there that was not so nice by half as the country butter. Here were brought, of a Saturday evening, all the rotten and half rotten fish, musk melons, water melons, peaches, et cetera that had not been sold at the earlier markets and which would be a mass of hopeless fruitrescence by Monday.

Brazen lunged salesmen at the fish stands would keep on shouting with ceaseless reiteration, "Get 'em fresh, get 'em while they last—only a few more left—strictly fresh fish, only five cents a pound," etc., etc.

Here could be seen of a Saturday evening in summer husky men, matrons and kids recklessly indulging in the joys of life by investing in five cent slices of watermelons or purchasing a whole melon and gorging on it within the precincts of the Capitol park, leaving the rinds strewn over benches and walks to the intense disgust of the park policemen. Nor were melon rinds the only debris left in the park by these banqueters from the State street market. Whisky flasks and a miscellaneous litter were what greeted the sight of the early Sunday morning stroller around the Capital buildings.

The customers at State street market have been a variable lot. The colored population was always much in evidence. Then came a time when the Hebrew denizens of the vicinity became a factor. More recently, as Huns, Slavs, Polacks

This unnamed alley ran behind the State Street Market. The tall smoke stacks probably belonged to the Harrisburg Electric Light Company or the Harrisburg Steam Heat and Power Company. (HSDC)

and what-not have settled in masses along Seventh street and other thoroughfares of the city, the market house has become a veritable congress of nations. Thrifty women of a dozen European lands, in their odd raiment, with heads bandaged with checkered handkerchiefs, can be seen providing for the Sunday feast that marks a day off from the unceasing grind of daily toil.

But the State Street market with all its bizarre sights will soon be a thing of the past.

The State Street Market House actually fronted on North Fourth Street, across from the capitol. The National Hotel is visible behind the market. (HSDC)

25. A Model Hotel in the "Old Eighth"

I have already spoken of some hotels, past and present, in the "Old Eighth," and will mention a few more before this series ends, but, for the present, I direct the reader's attention to a landlord of the Ward, now resting beneath the sod, whose fame deserves at least a passing tribute.

There have been drinking places in the "Old Eighth" associated with much that was shady and disreputable. Deeds were done in them that would not look well or read well beneath the light of publicity. This came, probably, to some extent, from the character of the people on whom they depended for patronage; and, conversely, the drinking places themselves had something to do with making many of the inhabitants of the Ward dissolute and needy derelicts.

But, knowing the reputation of the "Old Eighth" as you do, would you ever look to it to furnish the model saloon of the town? Yet there it was, a drinking place as strictly conducted as any that has ever existed in Harrisburg. That it was so was all due to the sterling character of the man who managed it.

That man was Frank McCabe. His father, Owen McCabe, also an olden time Harrisburg hotel keeper, was regarded, in his day, as the strongest man in Harrisburg; and some of his marvelous feats, as related by Capt. Levi Weaver and others of a past generation, have never been equaled, probably, in our community.

The son, Frank McCabe, in his earlier years, found employment on the towpath, as indeed did almost half the youngsters of that day, in Harrisburg. Frank McCabe did not know what fear was. When not imposed on he was the most peaceable and gentle of men, but, like his sire, Owen McCabe, and like every true son of the Emerald Isle, he would stand up for his rights and all his rights till the last horn blew.

Traversing the towpath at a day when some of the captains were brutal and many of their employees were bullies, young McCabe soon had the opportunity of choosing between submission to brutal abuse and showing the stuff that was in him; and he did the latter so effectively that, in a few years, his name was a

Carr's Restaurant at 602 Walnut Street, near the corner of Walnut and Filbert Streets, was covered in posters telling that Vogel's Big City Minstrels would be performing at the Majestic Theater, and then two days later they would be showing The Round Up. *(PSA)*

synonym for prowess from Elmira to the Chesapeake; and for many years after he had abandoned the mule-power freight trains of the unsalted water, his feats of courage were rehearsed in the legends of the boatmen along the Susquehanna and the Juniata.

McCabe as Landlord

After keeping hotel on South Second street and on Chestnut, Frank McCabe secured a license for an old hotel stand at the corner of North and Filbert streets, long known as the Kehl property. He was certainly the most independent landlord the "Eighth" has ever known. Again and again, his barroom would be the scene of a little conversation like this:

"I'll take a little whiskey, if you please."

"No, you won't. Not at this bar."

"Why, Frank, I'm sober."

"Don't care if you are. I don't want your custom, drunk or sober."

"But, I'm perfectly sober, Frank. I haven't taken a drink today."

"Well, keep it up for a few days more and you'll feel better and look better. If you haven't had a drink today, trot right off home and go to bed before you get any of the stuff inside of you."

"But I don't owe you anything. I have the money to pay for the drink."

110

"Then buy bread for your family."

"We have enough to eat in the house."

"Then buy your wife a new dress. God knows she needs one, the way she looked the other day when she passed here."

And Frank McCabe, the man who could talk thus, and did it, not once or twice, but repeatedly, prospered in business, while along State street, at the same time, were saloon keepers who would sell to every sot who had the price as long as he could totter to the bar, and yet were obliged to borrow money yearly with which to lift their licenses.

PROUD OF HIS DEMOCRACY

There was but one thing that this independent Eighth Ward hotel keeper was proud of, and that was that he was a Democrat all wool and a yard wide. In those days of Democratic factions and divisions, Frank McCabe never claimed to be a Breckenridge Democrat nor a Douglas Democrat, a Wallace Democrat nor a Randall Democrat, a Buckalew Democrat, a Bigler Democrat—but just a plain, every-day-and-all-the-time Democrat, without any frills, flounces or furbelows, who voted the ticket straight, the whole ticket and nothing but the ticket.

In recognition of his fealty to Democracy, his political associates several times urged him to be a candidate for some office, but he said to them, "Nay," and he said it emphatically.

The Rosebud Café sold Helmar cigarettes at the intersection of Walnut and Filbert Streets. (HSDC)

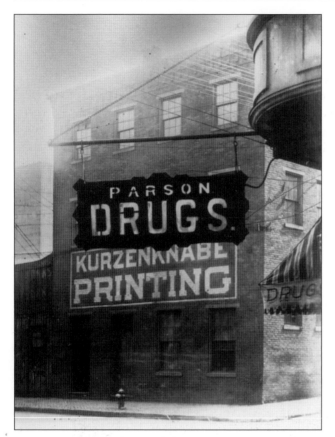

Kurzenknabe Printing had once occupied the corner building at Short and South Streets, but at this time it was the site of the E.N. Cooper Foundry. Kurzenknabe still does business in Harrisburg. (HSDC)

How One Gang Found Trouble

Once, without his knowledge, Frank McCabe was named for precinct assessor. A few hours later one of the rounders of the Eighth Ward came stalking into his bar room. He was one who was regarded as a bad man either with or without a gun— a leader in the notorious State street bridge gang, who had a record so malodorous that quiet and reputable citizens sought the other side of the street when they saw him sailing along on the war path. On this particular evening, when he sought Frank McCabe, he seemed to be reeking with disreputableness and whiskey.

"Goin' to put up a keg," was the tough's abrupt query. "The other candidates are all doin' it."

"Naw," was Frank McCabe's answer, and the word had a very authentic ring.

"If you don't," retorted the applicant for free booze, "what we'll do to you will be aplenty."

You see that youth had never been on the canal and knew naught of its legends.

"What's that?" demanded the landlord with that particular sibilant intonation, which any of his acquaintances will recall, but which defies description.

The reply was given yet more offensively.

McCabe spoke the tough never a word, but grasped a handy shillalah (and it was as beautiful a stick for peacemaking as one would wish to see) and started around the bar as rapidly as his game leg would permit.

The man who wanted to exercise the inalienable rights of a free American citizen by levying contributions on candidates, hesitated a moment. Three or four of his comrades were standing close behind him to see the result of his mission.

"Better git," suggested one. "He's a terror, and I am goin' now while the goin' is still good." The bridge gang man wavered a moment. Then he took good advice and did "git." And it was six months before he plucked up enough courage to pass down Frank McCabe's side of the street.

This 1904 photograph looks from Cowden Street west up South Street. The sign on the north side advertises a public sale of shoes, clothing, and stoves at 504 South. The sidewalk is brick and there is a fire hydrant, both signs of urban progress, but the street is still all dirt. (PSA)

113

26. Long Established Business Houses. Keeley Institute and St. Clare Infirmary. An Humble Heroine of Humanity.

May 12, 1913

The Capitol park extension will blot out a number of business houses which have been so long in one location under practically one management that they have become landmarks of that section.

I can mention but a few of the most prominent of these—and that very briefly.

In September 1864, Calvin Etter and James Shanklin, under the firm name of Etter & Shanklin engaged in the grocery business at the corner of State and Filbert streets in the building occupied in recent years by the Day Nursery. Eight years later the firm built at State and Cowden streets one square west of the former location, and there the business has been ever since, the leading grocery and feed store of the "Old Eighth."

Mr. Shanklin died in the early eighties of the last century, the business being continued by his surviving partner who in recent years has associated with him in the firm, his son Ross Etter.

George Orth, the popular grocer and baker, has been in business on State street, 26 years, of which time 20 years have been spent at this commodious location at the corner of State and West street.

In August 1877, Thomas A. Thorley started the drug business at 449 State street. In the 37 years which have intervened drug stores have come and drug stores have gone in the Old Eighth. Sometimes they flourished for a time like a green bay tree, then withered and disappeared.

But in all those years Thorley kept on the even tenor of his way, his store ever growing in popularity and patronage, an illustration, perhaps, of the Darwinian theory of the survival of the fittest.

Eastview, on the corner of North Fourth and North Street, was formerly the Keeley Institute. (HSDC)

THE KEELEY INSTITUTE

Probably the handsomest private residence in the Capitol Park extension district is the one erected, many years ago, by James Russ at the corner of Fourth and North streets, the building of which is said to have involved an expense approximating $30,000. Old residents will remember when the elevated bluff at this corner was occupied by a neat and quaint little two-story brick edifice with windows of the colonial order. Russ bought the property from the Herr estate.

Soon after the erection of the new building it was leased to some gentleman for the purpose of establishing a hospital for the treatment of persons addicted to the liquor or drug habit. Hence it became known as the Keeley Institute because the methods employed comprised the celebrated "Gold Cure," recently promulgated by Dr. Keeley, a system of treatment then in the height of its popularity and attracting popular attention in all parts of the land.

The Keeley Institute in this building was opened in June, 1892, with W.S. Thomas as manager and W.J. Reinhard as resident physician. After some years the institute was removed, for a time, to a large residential structure at North and Capital streets, where Joseph J. Kane was one of the resident physicians.

About 1901, however, the Institute returned to its original location in the Russ property, W.G. Haskell replacing Mr. Thomas as manager with John M. Raunick as physician in charge. At a later period, C.M. Rank was manager for a time, and

115

The James Russ house (the Keeley Institute) is on the right in this photograph of the corner of North Street and West Alley, looking south toward oncoming horses. On the left is a store selling tobacco and soft drinks. (HSDC)

still later Dr. Raunick had entire charge of the building in both the executive and medical lines.

After the discontinuance of the Keeley Institute in Harrisburg, the building was occupied for a time as a boarding house. It was amongst the earliest of the Eighth Ward properties to pass into the possession of the State, and the new Capitol being already overcrowded and additional room being needed for some of the departments, a bureau of one of them was transferred to it. Thus for a time at least, this fine structure has been saved from the general demolition that is going on all around it.

St. Clare Infirmary

During the years which elapsed between the first and second occupancy of the Russ house by the Keeley Institute it was the home of an excellent hospital conducted by the Sisters of Mercy, under the supervision of that Noble and devoted woman, Mother M. Clare, superioress of the order in Harrisburg.

During the Spanish-American war when Camp Meade was in existence contiguous to our city and typhoid fever was fearfully rife there through the imperfect sanitation of the camp and the carelessness or incompetence or both of some of the army officials in charge, the grand work of this St. Clare Infirmary became especially conspicuous. Many a stricken soldier had reason to bless its shelter and thank God for the ministering care of those devoted Sisters of Mercy. Mother Clare now rests beneath the low green tent toward which we are all tending, but I would be recreant to my duty, if, in this connection, I did not place a wreath of recognition and laudation on her tomb.

Humble Heroine of Humanity

To prevent any possible misapprehension, I wish to say again, most emphatically, that, although disgraceful vice conditions were in evidence, year after year, in the "Old Eighth," yet has it always been the home of many devoted and noble men and women whose unsullied lives shine all the more brightly by the contrast.

One of those whose whole life was a sermon, a benediction of good (I desire now to speak most briefly) was an humble colored woman living in a plainly furnished second story room on South alley near Spruce street. Day after day,

This was the view looking north up West Avenue from South Street. (HSDC)

117

night after night, there arose to her humble home the sounds of brawling and carousing of drunkenness and profanity, as men and women of the baser sort hooted and blasphemed on adjacent corners. With the love of God in her heart and deep faith in the future, year after year, she kept her sunny way, working and praying for those around her sunk in the depths of degradation and sin. She pled with the wayward, she organized juvenile temperance societies, she aided the victims of their own lusts as far as her slender means would permit. She never complained and she never lost heart. And thus through a long life she went on her unostentatious way, a guide to the sorely tempted, a blessing to the fallen.

She now rests, in Lincoln cemetery, beneath one of those tents whose curtains never outward swing; but the good accomplished by humble Annie E. Amos will be unfolded only by eternity.

There are women still living in the Eighth Ward who have led the same lives of rectitude that made the life of Mrs. Annie E. Amos a crown of glory. When they, too, go to their reward, may there be someone to place a garlanded tribute on their tombs.

"Honor and shame from no condition rise; Act well your part, there all the honor lies."

This view shows two men at work in the yard at Cooper's Foundry. The difference between the new capitol and its surroundings is dramatic, so much so that the decision to clear the Eighth probably seemed the obvious thing to do. (PSA)

27. WHITE SLAVERY IN THE "OLD EIGHTH"

MAY 19, 1913

A prominent character in one of Charles Dickens' works disposed of all cases of want, suffering, misery or oppression of the poor by denying that such things existed in England, ever had existed or ever would exist. Thus it was that a past age disposed of what is now spoken of, euphemistically, as "White Slavery." It was ignored entirely. It must not be alluded to.

Not so, today. Statesmen and philanthropic workers, leaders political and ecclesiastical recognize the gruesome facts in regard to the existence of commercialized vice in every civic center, and the menace which it is to national vitality and moral growth. It is made the subject of investigations and reports, or remedial legislation and critical study.

Vice conditions in the "Old Eighth" during the time that a considerable area there was given up to it, did not differ materially from what it was then, or is today, in any of the plague spots of our great cities. In all there is the same sordid greed, on the part of those from whom conscience has been seared, to make money from the ruin of the bodies and souls of their fellows. In all there is the same heartlessness, the same tales of woe and misery, the same unavailing wailings of remorse from the victims of iniquitous social systems.

THOSE WHO CONDUCTED DENS

The Harrisburg houses of commercialized vice in the past were not confined to the Eighth Ward, but those here located were so prominent and so melodious that they attained a more than State-wide notoriety. They were typical of all the others.

Here, for years, could be found the woman, grown old in sin, who seemed to take a fiendish delight in parading the main business streets, side by side with some young and handsome girl recently enmeshed in the net of evil. This woman, not originally a denizen of the Eighth, sought its protective environment when forced from a residential district. Once, in a specially distressing case of suffering and misery which came to a girl of tender years, a victim of the system, she was appealed to thus by an indignant woman striving to alleviate the sorrows of the unfortunate and the erring—"Have you no conscience? No heart? No Mercy for this girl?" "No," was the callous reply, "I have no heart, no conscience, no mercy. I do not know what they mean." After a long career marked by the blasted lives of others, alone and unattended, this woman was one day found dead in her house in the heart of the Eighth Ward's tenderloin. The only other occupant of the house was also dead. No mortal ever knew the conditions under which ghastly death stalked unbidden into that dwelling.

Hideous tragedies have been frequent in the Eighth Ward's purlieus of vice,—horrible and heartrending tragedies of which sometimes a little outline crept into the papers, but oftener the busy world jogged on, all unconscious of ruined lives and blasted reputations, sacrificed on the altar of ephemeral pleasure, which had turned to bitter ashes of Sodom on the lips of the participants. So many of these tragedies happened in the house just referred to, as rolled along the years, that it was characterized some years ago, in a Harrisburg newspaper, as "the house of tragedies."

The keepers of "White Slave" dens of the olden time in the Eighth Ward were of many types, but all of them of a bad type. Some places maintained a gaudy show of tinseled splendor, whilst others were but squalid ranches of the lowest type on narrow alleys, but in all these were the same tales of ruined lives, blasted reputations, debaucheries, remorse, despair.

Here were both men and women who sold their own daughters to lives of licentiousness and misery. Here were women who, fallen themselves, tried to blacken and deface whatever of your [words missing] . . . or innocence they could grasp within their withering influence.

Here have dwelt women, of enticing face and pleasing manners who have allured business and professional men of Harrisburg and other places from a life of rectitude and their own homes, until, reputation gone and money all squandered, bankrupt financially and morally, they were ignominiously ignored by the sirens who had lured them to ruin. Some of these men, shabby and needy, wandered for years as derelicts on our streets, or were wave-tossed flotsam and jetsam of life in the larger cities to which they had wandered in a vain hope of retrieving fortune. Most of them lost heart and went to dishonored graves; few of them ever made good again.

Here were women presiding over houses of sin who made a specialty of exciting the passions and pandering to the baser lusts of mere boys who were incited to steal from parents or employers that their orgies might be continued.

Here were houses where the deft-fingered panel thief operated with the connivance of the proprietress, who received the lion's share of the booty. Here were houses devoted to blackmail into which men of prominence were allured only to be confronted by a furious husband, manufactured for the occasion, who was vociferous in his demand for gore, but who could be placated by a comfortable cash consideration. In the long ago, one such victim, very high in the

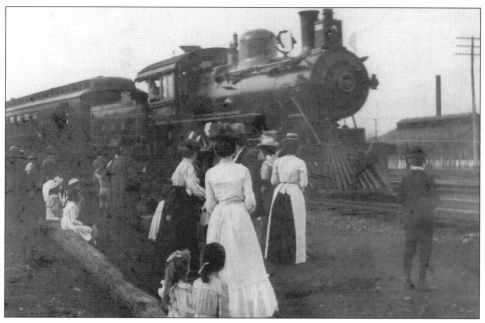

President William McKinley's funeral train passed by North Street and the Eighth Ward when it came through Harrisburg on September 16, 1901.

politics of the State, laid down a cool $500, a gold watch and other jewelry to purchase silence. Afterwards, when convinced he had been egregiously swindled, he did not dare to court the publicity of a prosecution, and on all this the swindlers who fixed up the scheme to bleed him, had counted.

VICTIMS OF THE SYSTEM

There is no class of humanity to whom life presents a more rayless and hopeless outlook than that the members of which, through the baseness and cupidity of man or their own folly, have been entrapped as slaves of a system which once flourished in the "Old Eighth." The life has been painted as one of pleasure. When too late they find it one of horror, remorse, degradation, disease and death.

The victims of the Eighth Ward dens were of many classes. Here came to hide her shame, the trusting girl who had been basely deceived. Here came recruits from every rural community of Central Pennsylvania who had sought the lure of city life by gaining employment in domestic service or factories. There were bad women at hand to counsel them not to be too straight-laced, and to act as guides in having a jolly time. There were bad men at hand to sap insidiously the precepts of virtue inculcated at a mother's knee.

Here came from other cities women who felt the fires of lust and depravity run riot in their veins, and sought some distant tenderloin. One woman of this class, long in "the Eighth," abandoned a luxuriant home and an indulgent husband in a

121

city of the Atlantic seaboard to consort with the lowest blacks and whites of the alleys of that Ward. She died a horrible death, the mystery of which was never explained, whether it was an accident of a drunken debauch or murder.

Nor were all the women of the Eighth Ward tenderloin of an illiterate class. Here have been, from time to time, beautiful girls of families high on the social list of New York and Boston, who had defied home trammels and gone forth on wild escapades.

"White Slavery," in its fullest sense is not peculiar to the present. There always were the "Old Eighth" brutes in the form of men, who lived in laziness on the sinful earnings of women whom they beat and abused, but it is only in recent years that these libels in the form of man are getting their deserts from the law.

Some of the dens of the "Eighth" have been leveled. The rest will soon follow. Could the materials of these buildings speak, from every time-stained timber, from every inch of plastering would come a tale of sorrows, agonies, debaucheries, remorses appalling in their horrors.

Could all the iniquities, the suicides, the sufferings these Eighth Ward dens have witnessed in half a century and more, be thrown into a panoramic view, there is not a young girl of our land, when tempted to depart from a life of rectitude, who would not shrink from the thought with horror, after one glance at the canvas.

The buildings which housed the Eighth Ward traders in bodies and souls are disappearing. Would God that the whole foul system they once typified might be swept with equal ease from all our land.

The view west from the far east end of Walnut Street at the Pennsylvania Railroad tracks. (HSDC)

28. A Monument to Filial Love: Fond Memories Evoked as Old Structures Fall

May 26, 1913

I dislike to think of the tearing down of one house in the Capitol Park Extension district, for round it clusters a blessed memory of a noble act nobly done. The United States would be a much poorer and weaker land today, had it never had the benefits arising from the brawn, bravery and brains of the millions of Irish and their descendants who made their home in this land of the free. And my story today is the story of a true-hearted Irishman, who, as a lad, played in the streets of Harrisburg, gained some scanty schooling, and then went west to woo fortune. His name was Isaac McConnell.

He reached the Rocky Mountain States just when the silver mines, which made many multi-millionaires, were in their incipient development. He became allied with some of the bonanza princes and fortune smiled on him beyond his wildest dreams or hopes.

And then Isaac McConnell hied himself back eastward. Prior to 1840 his hard working father secured a little plot of ground on what is now Fourth street, and had erected there an humble frame dwelling in which to shelter his family. There Isaac had been born, and there his widowed mother still dwelt with not any too much of this world's goods that she could call her own.

But Isaac McConnell, like a true Irishman, had never forgotten that mother; and now, as soon as wealth had crowned his labors, he spent an entire summer in Harrisburg superintending his labor of love. The old frame was quickly leveled and in its place rose a stately and capacious mansion, costing some $10,000, and superior in appearance to almost anything that could then be seen in that portion of the city.

Then McConnell furnished the house throughout, not only comfortably, but luxuriously, adorned it with costly paintings for which he paid a considerable price, and installed his mother in the new residence which to her presented the

Isaac McConnell's house, built for his mother, was at 143 Fourth Street near the intersection of Cranberry Alley and Fourth Streets. (HSDC)

splendor of a palace. Then leaving her with ample means for her declining days, the dutiful son again betook himself to the new El Dorado in the ravines of the Rockies. The mother is dead and all the McConnell family except Isaac himself. The costly paintings, or some of them at least, are in the possession of a niece in Washington, D.C. The recollection of the other who once lived on Fourth street in the house just described has become a misty memory, and soon the building will be demolished. But I have done what in me lay to perpetuate the noble deed of the Irish lad that revered his mother.

For years the building, 143 Fourth street, has been a boarding house. A talented school teacher, Miss Minnie A. Shaffer, having found her health declining under the strain of school work, came to Harrisburg, found the house a most eligible location for entertaining boarders, and, making a success of her new venture from the first, has gained renewed physical vigor.

SEVERING OF HEART TIES

I have spoken in some numbers of this series of the demolition of buildings, every timber of which, if gifted with speech, could tell of crime and debauchery. There is a brighter side to the picture. Around many time-stained buildings of the old "Eighth" cling blessed memories which are stored in the hearts of those who, as children, there knew a mother's love and a father's care.

In refreshing my mind as to the data in regard to the house that Isaac McConnell built, I called on Miss Annie Glancy, 133 North Fourth street, an intimate acquaintance of the McConnells'. The house in which she resides was built by her father in 1846. There Miss Glancy was born and there she passed her entire life. Each room of that house has become a shrine around which cluster fond memories of the dear departed. Think you, Miss Glancy and others similarly situated can leave those homes without many a pang?

VISITED HOME OF CHILDHOOD

Some months ago a well dressed lady rapped on the door of one of the frames standing on the lower side of State street, a short distance west of Filbert. To the woman who opened the door, she said, "Please, madam, could I come into your house and rest a moment."

The lady of the house, supposing that the applicant had been taken ill suddenly on the street, graciously accorded permission and brought the stranger a glass of water. After gazing eagerly around the room the visitor said in a voice trembling with emotion: "Madam, excuse this intrusion. In this house I was born; here I knew the fond care of a loving father; here I lisped my first prayers at my mother's knees; here in happy childhood I played with brothers and sisters, some of whom now sleep in the low, green tents. Every nook in this weather-battered building is to me like a sacred sanctuary. I hear all these houses are to be destroyed soon, and I have come to Harrisburg to see once more the home of my infancy ere it disappears forever."

The lady of the house courteously escorted her visitor through it. As memory after memory was evoked in the several rooms, tears more than once welled up unbidden to the eyes of the one traversing her old home.

Ninety-three years ago Isaac Tomlinson started a factory in a frame building on Walnut street, where now stands the Fager schoolhouse, building stages for the Calder transportation lines. In a few years he removed to a plot of 80 by 210 feet extending from Walnut street to the railroad, where now stands the Witman-Schwarz wholesale house. Later the business descended to his son, John B. Tomlinson, who resided in the State street frame building, just spoken of, from 1849 to 1876. It was a daughter of John B. Tomlinson, a sister of Isaac Tomlinson, of Forster street, Prof. John K. Tomlinson, deceased, of the Harrisburg High School faculty, and William Tomlinson, deceased, long a Court House employee, who had made the visit, just narrated, to the home of her childhood.

Memories of a similar character will give at least a passing pang to many a heart, as house after house of the "Old Eighth" passes into oblivion.

A PAIR OF PATRIOTIC YOUTHS

The same frame building of the "Old Eighth" contributed on one occasion, at least, to the jollity of the Ward. At the outbreak of the Civil War, in 1861, immediately after the rioting in Baltimore, all sorts of wild rumors gained credence. Harrisburg as near the border line was, for weeks, the center of a chronic excitement.

One evening a disciple of Ananias and his spouse Sapphira, came panting into Harrisburg with the information that 10,000 toughs from Baltimore were on the march to sack and burn Harrisburg. They were just across the river; he had seen the vanguard himself. Instantly there was turmoil and uproar in Harrisburg, and a hurrying to and fro.

At that day almost every house was well supplied with firearms. John B. Tomlinson had a fair share of rifles and fowling pieces around his premises. Two of the Tomlinson youths quickly came to the conclusion that if the Baltimoreans were marching on Harrisburg, they must be exterminated at all hazards; and, moreover, that they were the lads to turn the trick. So collecting all the firearms about the premises and entrenching themselves in the second story, they began a furious fusillade, riverward, from the windows, that made life in the Eighth Ward strenuous for some minutes, as the bullets went whizzing along the streets.

People a few squares away from the volleys that came from Tomlinson's windows were thrown in wild alarm by the supposition that the invaders had already captured the town by a flank movement and that the carnage was on, in all its horrors.

This winsome photograph was labeled the "North Street Boys," but the little fellow with the silk tie looks like he should be playing with the more proper Front Street Crowd. (HSDC)

29. How a Youth, Fond of Experiments, Made Things Lively in the Old Eighth; The Industrial Plan That Edward Moeslein Founded

June 2, 1913

There have been all kinds of lively times in the Old Eighth. In former days when the lumber raft "Yankees" roamed over there and attempted to take the "Red Lion" by storm, or stretched their stalwart forms on the flat cellar doors of State street to sleep off their debauches, they made it interesting for all they encountered. The "Bridge Gang," when on the war path, gave many a citizen the creeps.

When 500 or so of the soldiers, who were being paid off in 1865, came into the Ward of a Sunday on a hunt for rum and excitement, it was lively. It has often been lively around State and Spruce or along South street, of a Saturday while razors gleamed and brickbats filled the air. But I do not intend to catalogue all the Eighth Ward entertainments of half a century. The list is too long a one.

But about the biggest farce and free-for-all show the Eighth Ward ever had was started by a bit of a kid who had a fondness for experiments and who would not take a dare. Our forefathers, in their wisdom, built a massive iron fence around the Capitol park. This was put up from time to time in sections, part of the fence being cast at the Bay foundry, State and Canal streets, and part at the Jennings foundry, Short and South streets. This fence was intended to keep out the cattle and swine which then roamed the mud thoroughfares of the borough, but was strong enough to defy elephants.

One day an urchin, son of a prosperous Eighth Ward landlord, was told by one of his companions that he could not get his head between two of the massive bars fixed perpendicularly in the longitudinal metallic rails. The youth did the trick

This is the back of the Cooper Foundry, on Tanner's Alley. The tower of Saint Lawrence Catholic Church is in the background at the left. By this time this photo was taken, the adjoining Steam Heat and Power Company had been demolished. (PSA)

with ease and then lost the combination, for he could not get his head out. No dog fight ever drew an immense audience half so quickly as did the yells of that boy. The Ward turned out, en masse, at the signal, and last of all the rather portly father came puffing up to the scene of action.

Now that father was the champion stutterer of the village of that day, and the way he fractured the English language as he strove to express the thoughts which arose in him on this occasion, would give any self-respecting linotype machine the quinsy in attempting a reproduction, so I'll not write it down.

WARD ENJOYS THE FREE SHOW

Then the father thought a moment, returned to his nearby hostelry and came back, on the jump, armed with an ax which he poised for a frantic blow on the imprisoning bar. Had he struck the mass of iron tightly wedged against the youth's neck, even an ordinary idiot could easily tell what would have happened to the boy. A man in the crowd caught the father's arm ere the blow descended, and then the landlord turned on the interferer.

At it they went, hammer and tongs. There was not much science in the "mill," but there was plenty of ginger and a fair supply of "claret."

While the two were battling to a finish, some of the crowd, now numbering hundreds, had succeeded in dislodging one of the heavy irons from its socket, thus relieving the young American in the case. By the time the son was out of chancery, the father was so thoroughly pummeled that it occurred to him it would be advisable to pick some one nearer his left. Just then he caught a glimpse of the youthful cause of the whole circus, and he reached for him viciously, the while the words which exploded from him in volcanic stutters were deeply tinged with profanity.

The boy probably thought the old man was too excited then to listen to reason. Accordingly he departed Walnut street way, and he departed with great rapidity. In less than half a second a racing carnival down Fourth street was on that had any six-day, go-as-you-please New York walking match looking tamer by comparison than a snail's promenade. The hundreds of boys and most of the men of the assemblage joined in the procession. It was a free show and their appetite was whetted for all the fun in sight.

Presently the father collided with a fat man coming up the street. It was a bad spill and, as the two gathered themselves from the wreckage, the conversation of both had ultra-sulphurous trimmings. The kid knew a providential interference when he saw it, and the way he dug through the dust and street litter down Cranberry and Tanner was a whole poem in twelve cantos on the word agility.

Great Industrial Plant on State Street

In a recent number of this series I spoke of the vast benefits conferred on America by the Irish emigration which came to its shores. Equally great are the advantages which we have derived from the influence from Germany. Pennsylvania, in particular, has been wonderfully developed by the sturdy Germans and their descendants. We have had many conspicuous examples in Harrisburg amongst whom Edward Moeslein ranks high. He has been a man of many and ceaseless activities, having been allied with and pushed forward many industries which have contributed to the financial upbuilding of the city. Even a brief summary of these would not be germane to the purposes of this paper, except as some of them lie within the zone of Capitol Park extension. Despite all these varied activities, Mr. Moeslein has always found time to mingle actively in public and municipal affairs.

Some fifteen years ago Mr. Moeslein erected an industrial building at 414-416 State street intended for the occupancy of the Capital City Shoe Manufacturing Co., which had been organized, some years before, with William C. Gorgas as president; Henry J. Beatty, secretary and treasurer; Edward Moeslein, manager; and John E. Bickel, superintendent. This industry had been housed originally at Jennings Foundry building, 138 Short street.

About 1900 this industry was replaced in the new building by the Gordon Manufacturing Co., engaged in making rubber collars and cuffs, which was removed later to a building erected specially for its use, a short distance away, which extended from State street to North alley. Still later the collar and cuff industry, with some changes in ownership, was transferred to the large building on Walnut street, near the P.R.R., which extends to South street, but still within the boundaries of the proposed park extension. Through all these years, the

Gordon Manufacturing Co., has continued to be a prominent factor in the city's industrial work. Following the Gordon Co., a flour sack factory was opened in the new State street plant, which is now in a flourishing condition on one of the thoroughfares of hustling Allison's hill.

ENLARGEMENT OF THE STATE STREET PLANT

Two names that have been extensively associated with laundry interests in Harrisburg are W.E. Orth and Charles A. Klemm. Years ago there were various sales and transfers of business between these two, who for a time were partners, and various purchases of other laundries which it would not be profitable to follow up here in detail. From these gradually grew up W.E. Orth's City Star Laundry. This business, located for a number of years in the old Jennings building, 138 Short street, had grown to such proportions that about ten years ago Mr. Orth purchased the State street building to which he has since made two extensive additions, making it one of the largest and most finely equipped industrial plants in Harrisburg. It now extends from 414 to 418 State street and along west to North Alley.

The Gordon Manufacturing Company was on the corner of Filbert and Walnut Streets. The sign facing Walnut says they made rubber collars and cuffs. (PSA)

This view of the opposite side of the Gordon Company shows that the Paxton Flour and Feed Company and the Harrisburg Storage Company were nearby. (PSA)

On the second floor of this immense building, C.M. Thomson, for years, conducted the Glen Manufacturing Co., engaged in making infants' shoes, which is still in the same location owned by Mr. Moeslein and others. On the Third floor, the ever youthful John C. Jennings, who has now associated his son Edwin D., in business with him, manufactures various articles of ladies apparel. In the northern annex to the building is Moeslein's Harrisburg Apparel Co., with the courteous Alonso G. Lehman as manager.

I am informed that the amount disbursed as wages to the employees in the various industries of the building exceeds $2,300 weekly.

30. An Episode from Lafayette Hall That Was Staged in the Police Court

June 9, 1913

An early number of this series told somewhat of Lafayette hall. Comparatively few of the persons who were victimized in the various Eighth Ward resorts ever aired their grievances before the public. I will give the story of one man who visited Lafayette hall and then told his tale of woe in the police court in the days when Mayor Boas presided there, as typical of the experience of many a man who has wandered into the olden time Eighth Ward haunts.

Among the suckers who sought amusement in Harrisburg almost 40 years ago, was a certain frisky individual who claimed to be from the capitol city of "Alt Berks" and that his name was Wiseman. The first statement may have been correct, for some Reading men, when turned loose, are liable to wander into all sorts of places. However, that is no specialty of the city of pretzels, for there are plenty of Harrisburg men ditto.

As to the traveler's second claim, I am harassed with doubts—a whole encyclopedia of them. If the name was genuine, it was a misnomer. Wise men were not liable to plant their feet in the Lafayette hall of that day.

Be that as it may, the Reading man having stopped at a Market street hotel, told the porter he was a philanthropist and a student of social conditions, and that he desired to interview vice at close range, so as to be better prepared to suggest the proper remedial treatment.

Found Sociable Companions

Now most Harrisburg porters of that day were trade drummers for one or other of the rival establishments of classic East State street, and, naturally, never let an opportunity pass of clearing a dividend. So this particular porter took the Reading student of social conditions to Lafayette hall.

To the visitor both the hall and the frame annex to it looked peaceful and pleasant. He entered and drank wine and gin with those he met. There was quite a goodly company in the parlors, and they were all glad to see him. He could not recall when he had found more genial companionship. He assented to every proposition intended to make his stay in the Capitol City pleasant and one long to be remembered; and was forced to confess that vice at close range did not appear half as black as it had been painted.

After bidding all his new friends an affectionate and effusive farewell, the while he collared several more gins, the guest of the hour departed Reading-way with a light heart, only to discover, later, that his pocketbook which had contained $450, was yet lighter than his heart.

WISEMAN'S SECOND TRIP TO HARRISBURG

And then Mr. Wiseman came back hastily to Harrisburg, accompanied by two Reading detectives, and there was a seance at Mayor Boas' office, to which all parties in interest were invited, the cards to the sociable being delivered by men wearing blue clothing, ornamented with brass buttons.

The proprietor of the hall stately, immaculately dressed, attended; likewise his spouse; likewise certain damsels for whom street clothing had been hastily procured to replace the short dress and flashing which was the customary female uniform of East State street at that day. These damsels stated that their names were Frankie Best, Bertie Lee, Ettie Miller and the like. Being interrogated as to their

The corner of Walnut and Cowden Streets shows the store at 600 Walnut still open and selling ice cream, but what used to be the building across the street at 522 has been bought up and demolished. (PSA)

At Anna Shein's properties at 123 and 121 Cowden Street, smokers once had their choice of Polar Bear, Oasis, Piedmont, Havana Ribbon, or Union Leader tobacco. (PSA)

occupations, they one and all asserted with deep feeling that they were honest, hardworking women with an intense dislike for untruthfulness or depravity. One was a vest-maker, who daily plied the needle, and earned a plain but comfortable living with the sweat of her brow; one was an expert cook; while yet another was only a humble charwoman who scrubbed office floors for a livelihood. All had on their faces a sweet and sanctified look of guilefulness, mingled with amazement that any one should dare to harbor a thought that they would be guilty of any wickedness.

The proprietor, his wife, the damsels—all looked the Reading man over, carefully, thoughtfully, almost prayerfully. They knew him not. He had never graced their choice social circle. He was an utter stranger upon whom their eyes had never rested. They knew naught of the gin and the wine he had imbibed. They had never played eucher or any other game with him, for they considered card playing naughty. Evidently the man from Reading was under the hallucination of a pipe dream.

The wanderer from Reading repeated his tale of ill luck, but it threw no light on whither his wad had vanished. Some of the spectators at the hearing suggested he didn't know where he had been; some that he never had any money; and, again, others that he needed a guardian. The Reading chap has had plenty of imitators as rolled along the years, for the fools are never all dead at once. And the

134

biggest fools in the whole bunch are the gray-headed fools and the bald-headed fools when they go into their second dotage and get giddy.

A pretty close second to them are the gilded youth who, freed from home restraints, think the wild oats crop must be sown with lavish hand so that they will be classed as "good fellows and all round sports."

These two classes have kept the leeches of the Eighth Ward tenderloin and every other tenderloin of the United States in spending money and gorgeous apparel. Some of the money here squandered represented the cash withheld from defrauded creditors; some was coin stolen from employers; and (deepest shame of fallen manhood!) some of the means here spent have represented the ragged clothing and empty stomachs of the faithful wife and innocent children of men entranced by passion till shame had ceased to exist.

Some of the coin profusely scattered by the visitors to Eighth Ward dens was money legitimately their own, which, properly husbanded, would have given ease and affluence in future life. Recklessly wasted, it has made many a man, who started in life with fair prospects, a pauper, without the comforts of life in the winter of his age.

For in Harrisburg, and everywhere, now, and in the years of the past and the future, as truly as when St. Paul penned the lines—"The wages of sin is death."

This is a view of more of Anna Shein's properties at 119, 117, and 115 Cowden Street. (PSA)

31. Two Notable Fire Companies

June 16, 1913

Any account of the district about to be occupied by the extension to the Capitol Park that failed to speak of the two excellent companies of the Harrisburg Fire Department located within its limits, would be incomplete. During the life of these companies there have been wonderful changes in fire fighting methods and wonderful improvements in the machinery employed.

In point of age, the Citizen Company is the third one to be organized in the present Harrisburg Fire Department. It dates back to 1836, when Harrisburg, although the Capital of our State, was a mere country village. Its first officers were William Bostick, president; Henry Lyne, vice president; George S. Kemble, treasurer; and William Parkhill, secretary.

In the long ago, the borough of Harrisburg erected two one-story frame engine houses in the lower part of the Capitol grounds, contiguous to the long since abandoned High street and about opposite the present site of the Majestic Theatre. One of these was called the Harrisburg engine house. The other, quite close to it, was given for a time to the newly formed Citizen company, for its occupancy. Subsequently, however, a new building located in the grounds, but quite near to the Third and Walnut street entrance, was built for the use of the Citizen Company. This latter building was also a frame, but of considerable size, painted, and in other ways made quite tasty, according to the standard of that day. From this point, the company was transferred to its present location on Fourth street, just above Walnut.

Old Fire Fighting Machinery

The first engine purchased for the Citizen Company, is described in old records as a beautiful and powerful engine of second class capacity, throwing a gallery and two side streams. It was manufactured at the establishment of Joel Bates in Philadelphia and cost $950. In 1838, soon after the purchase of this engine, there were, in quick succession, two destructive fires in the vicinity of Fourth and Market streets, in one of which Zion Lutheran church was destroyed.

Old chronicles tell us that in these fires the new engine of the Citizen Company was fully tested and found of great value; for, being provided with a suction apparatus, it was able to draw water from the canal, thus doing away partially with the bucket lines.

As all this will probably sound very enigmatic to the majority of the readers of the present generation, it may be well to explain that we are now dealing with a time when every householder was required to keep, at a convenient place on his premises, at least two serviceable leathern buckets with his name painted on them. When a fire alarm was heard it was the duty of every man to grab his buckets and rush toward the conflagration. A double line of men, women and children was formed from the engine stationed near the burning building to some point from which water could be obtained.

Along one line were passed the filled buckets of water to be dumped into the tank attached to the engine. Along the other line, the emptied buckets were returned for refilling. Space will not permit me to enter into an explanation of the various complicated forms of machinery by which the water was projected upon the blaze. Some of the engines of that day were fearfully and wonderfully made.

Soon after the fires at Fourth and Market streets, water was introduced into the borough and hydrants were located at various points along the streets. Then hose replaced the bucket brigades, the Citizen being the first fire company in Harrisburg to use hose, having purchased 1,600 feet in Philadelphia. At the same time the company purchased the first hose carriage ever seen in Harrisburg, the price being $285.

This view from the intersection of Fourth and Walnut Streets toward the capitol shows the Citizens Fire House, the tall building in the middle of the block. (HSDC)

137

The Mt. Vernon Hook and Ladder Company was near North Alley on North Fourth Street. Firemen stand ready at the doorway. (HSDC)

CHARTERED 1841

The Citizen company was chartered in 1841. Later the discovery having been made that the charter was defective, a new constitution and by laws were adopted which were approved by the Dauphin county court, August 23, 1858.

In the fall of 1856, the company bought in Philadelphia a second hose carriage which took the town of that day by storm when exhibited on the streets. It was most handsomely mounted with silver and other embellishments and cost $1,000. Soon after, it is recorded that the company bought a handsome "spider" manufactured to order by R.J. Fleming of Harrisburg for $200.

The latest investment of the company in engines previous to obtaining a steam engine was in October 1858 when it bought a 3,500 lb. Button engine costing $2,050. It required 50 men to work it. Space will not permit the tracing of the company's history in recent years. It has always had an honorable record of efficiency and good service.

MT. VERNON COMPANY

The well known Mt. Vernon company was organized April 8th, 1858 and had a temporary location on Front street, but was soon removed to Locust street, between Third and Fourth streets, a section now known as Federal Square. After some years it was transferred to its present location on Fourth street above State.

Its first name was the Independent Hook and Ladder Company, but that title was only retained until August of the year of its organization when the term Mt. Vernon was substituted.

The first apparatus of the company was manufactured for it by R.J. Fleming of Harrisburg. It was considered very elegant and up-to-date according to the standards of that day, but, of course, was a mere toy along side of the magnificent apparatus with which the company is now equipped.

The Mt. Vernon company, from the time of its organization down to the present, has always been noted for the large number of prominent men who have been enrolled in its ranks. In its very first list of officials I find such names as William C.A. Lawrence, the first president; Richard B.A. Berkman, William B. Wilson, J.A. Carman, David C. May, Thomas W. Anderson, Frank A. Murray, Robert G. Denning, and T. Rockhill Smith, all men who were leaders in their various lines, in the Harrisburg of fifty-five years ago.

This rare photograph shows men operating the Harrisburg Light and Power Company's contraption for removing telephone poles on January 22, 1914. Autos are parked along the street, but there is still a drinking font for horses. (PSA)

32. "THE RED LION"

JUNE 23, 1913

In a previous number of this series it was stated that one of the licensed hotels now in existence on East State street was kept by a prominent colored man, Theodore Frye. This, however, has not been the only hostelry of the vicinage presided over by a negro. There have been several previous attempts in the "Old Eighth" to maintain a drinking place especially catering to colored trade, most of which have been of short duration.

One of the most prominent colored men in the business in the past was Larry McDonnell, who was located at a number of places, one of them being where the Hotel LeRoy now stands at State and Cowden streets. From here he moved to State street near North Fifth (Spruce), and, when burned out there, he occupied the adjacent corner, which is the present Frye stand after having, during the lapse of many years, a multiplicity of successive landlords. The well known barber, Charles Jackson, was also interested in some of the hotel ventures of past years.

BUILDING THE GARNER HOUSE

The first hotel of the Ward conducted by colored landlords was the Garner House, located at the south-west corner of South and Cowden streets, in the very heart of the congested district, where the network of streets was narrowest and most tortuous and where squalor and vice were always elbowing each other under living conditions that were disgraceful to our city.

When the ramshackle frame was torn down, some years ago, a kid reporter of one of our dailies announced in his paper that the building had attained the patriarchal age of ninety years.

It had not attained quite half that age, but, as far as concentrated wickedness goes, it had enough scored up against it to have been in existence since the day when Noah came out of the ark.

As I saw the shabby old timbers and flooring ripped up, it seemed as if, even in their very muteness, they bore testimony to witnessing about every crime, cruelty and grossness in the varied catalogue of sin. It was well they possessed no audible tongue of accusation for the drunkenness, the bestiality, the suicides, the bloody fights, the carouses, the nameless crimes, the robberies, the blasphemes, the tragedies of every class those old rooms had witnessed have generally passed to an oblivion that should remain unbroken.

It was built in 1865 by William Sible, for many years a very prominent man of affairs in Harrisburg. He was, at one time, an extensive real estate owner and erected many buildings in a local term for a portion of the Seventh Ward. Here are still standing long rows of frame structures which he built.

Two well known colored men of the city opened a hotel in the new building. These were William Battis, afterwards an alderman in the Eighth Ward, who died a few years ago in Middletown, and Alfred Garner, long a porter at the railway stations, who was found dead, but quite recently, in a Market street room.

It was from the latter that the house received its name, although, in after years, in common conversation and even in the columns of the dailies, the term was almost universally corrupted into "the Garnett House."

THE "RED LION"

The firm of Battis & Garner was not of long duration. Its members were not harmonious, and it was not a financial success—for one of them at least. A year or two later, Battis removed a square further west where he owned a property at the

This view of Cowden Street looks north from Walnut Street to South Street, where the notorious Red Lion saloon was located. (HSDC)

141

This 1909 photograph looks up the North Alley hill west toward the capitol. (PSA)

intersection of Short and South streets. At this place he conducted a well known hotel for a number of years.

Then the "Red Lion" became the successor of the not very much lamented "Garner House." I do not know that the latter, when in operation, ever presented any similarity to a Christian Endeavor convention; but its habitues were a very Quaker Seventh-day assemblage in comparison with those who held orgy at the sign of the "Red Lion." In the seventies of the last century, if a Harrisburger wanted to show a visiting sport from another city a gilded palace of sin, he took him to Lafayette Hall. But if he wanted to show the same visitor sin itself in concentrated form, without any ornamentation, flounces, or furbelows, he took him to the "Red Lion," and the visitor generally came away admitting that the Five Points of New York, or the Old Loun in Baltimore had nothing to beat it. The "Red Lion" had Canal street, Buffalo, or Bainbridge between Third and Fourth, Philadelphia down and out, even when these last-mentioned places were in their palmiest days of a vice career.

Bill of Fare at the "Red Lion"

There was not even a feeble attempt at the concealment of vice. It was flaunted openly, defiantly at all who passed along. In this very flaunting, studiedly paraded before the public, was the advertisement intended to bring dollars to the house. And the dollars flowed in rapidly, copiously.

It was a very wild Harrisburg, that Harrisburg of the later sixties and early seventies of the last century. It was a Harrisburg but little recovered from Camp Curtin days' demoralization. The strangers who passed through were numerous and many of them readily adapted themselves to the tone of the tenderloin of that day.

So at the Red Lion the revel ran fast and furious. It never ceased at night and seldom in the day, unless perchance, at very early hours of the morning. Blacklegs and crooks of every kind were amongst the roomers from time to time. As one became too well known to the authorities or pulled the trick that compelled a hasty departure another would take his place.

The exercises at the Red Lion 40 to 45 years ago were of a varied character, and often of a nature not calculated to tranquillize the nerves. When a female, "Lost to all her friends, her virtue fled," filling up with bad whiskey, dope, and remorse, begins to ponder on her days of innocence and the depths to which she has descended, those are liable to be very unwholesome fancies that go flitting multitudinously through her mind. Fancies would soon produce action and a promenade from cellar to garret in search of a scrap.

On one occasion a denizen of the Red Lion, arming herself with a hefty butcher knife, started amuck with the avowed intention of carving the entire

This 1904 photograph shows the proliferation of signs on Fourth Street across from the new capitol building. (PSA)

establishment and firing the castle to make a grand cremation of the corpses to save funeral expenses. Then, when the blaze was well started, she would give the victims of her revenge the merry "ha! ha?" and immolate herself. But the Red Lion whiskey on which she had loaded up was terribly swift in its effects and, between intoxication and hysteria, she was not able to inflict any very deep wound before she was overpowered.

A balcony in the rear of the building, hemmed in on all sides by other unsightly frame buildings and overlooking nothing in the way of scenery but the tiniest and filthiest kind of a yard, was a favorite place for all manner of satanic convocations and beastly revels. From it at least one man plunged to death.

You will hear yet somewhat more about the "Red Lion," and the why of it that this and other similar blots upon civic decency have been able to flourish in a city of churches.

This 1904 photograph shows South Alley before brick paving. (PSA)

33. "The Red Lion" at Its Lowest

June 30, 1913

A shabby specimen of architecture was the building which housed the "Red Lion" outfit, even at its best and newest.

It was built at a day when, with vast open expanses all around the city, it was a cardinal doctrine of all builders that every inch of ground must be occupied with buildings and none of it wasted in the foolishness of lawns, or flower beds, or yards of any character. As to the buildings themselves the absorbing thought was that the more rooms you place in a house, the more people can be packed into it; and the lower down you make the ceilings, the more stories you can get on the house at the least possible expense. Consequently, the building which flaunted the sign of the "Red Lion" was of cheap materials, of irregular dimensions and of a zigzag foundation line. Yet its outside was the best part of it, for the interior was a geometrical puzzle that no man ever solved. Its architectural monstrosities of rooms with no particular shape, labyrinthian halls, steep and narrow stairways, little nooks and fenced-off rooms at all sorts of angles, gave it a weird absurdity of appearance and lack of comfort which it never lost.

A Corpse at the "Red Lion"

Smallpox was a rather common thing in the Harrisburg of forty years ago. Sanitary boards and sanitary rules were not. I have seen men with the undried marks of the loathsome disease mingling nonchalantly with the crowds at the old Northern Central station, with no one to interfere or forbid it.

On one occasion an inhabitant of the Red Lion was taken with the disease. The revel stopped not for a moment. She was secluded in a stuffy little third-story room, where, it is to be surmised, her attention was of the scantiest.

In three days she died; and some time between midnight and morning, the corpse was bundled out of the building and stuck into the ground somewhere, without mourners or burial rights, whilst her clothing was converted into a bonfire in one of the hollows east of the city. The story was whispered around to many in the tenderloin, yet there never was official interference or investigation.

Pardon a moment's digression. I can't help it. That young girl! (I was told she was barely twenty years of age) was once an innocent child, the prattling pride of fond parents. Young girl tempted to stray from the path of right and virtue, remember the terse text, "The wages of sin is death." I have used the text before. It needs to be reiterated again and again if one would draw the proper moral from gruesome life in the tenderloin of the "Old Eighth."

One other thought. Any social or governmental condition that permits the existence of the life of which the "Red Lion" was typical, is rotten and defective somewhere. Civic betterment means more than fine buildings, clean streets, parks and playgrounds. It means also civic purity.

"Red Lion" vs. "Lafayette Hall"

In an early number of the series it was told how the man who built Lafayette Hall suddenly found himself outside of the breastworks by having his license application turned down by the Dauphin County Court. Cook was amazed,

This view of Cowden Street looks southeast from South Street to Walnut and beyond. The famous Red Lion Saloon was at the southwest corner of South and Cowden Streets, competing with Harry Cook's Lafayette Hall two blocks away at Fifth and State Streets. (HSDC)

146

stupefied. "Could such things be," he asked himself. "In this land of the free and home of the grafter?" To increase his indignation, the Red Lion still kept on the even tenor of its way as a place licensed by the great State of Pennsylvania to provide entertainment for man and beast.

Relations became strained between the proprietors of the rival joints. The story of a part of the proceedings ran thus. On a certain day, one who claimed to speak for authority higher up came to the Red Lion and spoke certain words unto the landlord. What he said was terse and emphatic. The place was wide open—very wide open—notoriously wide open. Certain men in authority could no longer stand for so flagrant a violation of good morals within the city of Harrisburg— unless there was something doing in a pecuniary line.

The landlord replied that he was painfully aware that the wide open allegation was strictly true. He himself was a man of strong moral impulses, but there were certain sons and daughters of Belial lodging at his place who scoffed at all his reproofs. It cut him to the soul to think how wicked they were and how they brought odium on his hotel. Yet he loved these same wicked people and would exhort them again and again. In the meantime he would come down with a handsome sum in hand and the promise of a fat monthly stipend to be duly and regularly paid to the go-between if that would assist disturbed authorities in looking in another direction when nosing around over Harrisburg's sin chart.

Flushed with success, the alleged agent of authority wended his way to Lafayette Hall. What Harry Cook spoke to him was not of a cheering character. He simply grasped a serviceable shillalah and moved around very rapidly to the front of his elegant marble bar at the same time inviting the interviewer to get out of that to the warmest place he knew of, and to do it very quickly. The alleged agent did not get out of that in a most indignified manner, but with great precipitation, for Harry Cook was not a man to be trifled with.

And from that day his troubles with the police seemed to spring up incessantly. He felt sore about the deal he was getting.

Booze Expert Finds Trouble

A general loafer around town who hung around the Red Lion a good bit as a sort of general utility man in doing all sorts of menial jobs for an occasional drink of rum and who had been a witness against several illegal liquor sellers that ran afoul of the ill-will of the police, strolled carelessly into Lafayette Hall one day and remarked, "I'll take a little whiskey Harry." Cook spoke him never a word, but, had the loafer been wise enough to scan his face, he would have seen the brewing of trouble. Coming swiftly from behind the bar the landlord of Lafayette Hall seized his would-be patron by the nape of the neck and the seat of his inexpressibles and chucked him clear down the flight of high stone steps and beyond the curb line into the dust of State street.

Of course there was a suit for assault and battery, and it cost Cook a pretty penny for his ten seconds of athletic exercise. He put all the blame on the

Poplar Street was the eastern boundary of that part of the "Bloody Eighth" scheduled for demolition. This view looks northward from the corner of Poplar and State Street. (HSDC)

proprietor of the Red Lion and the relations between the two became more tense and sulphurous than ever.

The Red Lion man, most likely, had nothing to do with the loafer's visit to Lafayette Hall. He was probably sent there by some one in police circles to act the "stool" for them as he had done in other areas in the past.

Tis said that the high and refined science of winking at vice for a consideration, and making it hot for those who don't pay up, has not become entirely a lost art, even at the present day, in some of the cities of the United States.

A Reformed Colored Citizen

On one occasion, in the dusk of evening, a stout female denizen of the Red Lion, after an all day wrestle with dope, bad whiskey, various brands of sin, and remorse, took a flying leap from the little balcony in the rear, presumably with suicidal intent.

In the few square feet beneath, sarcastically called a yard, one of the very fattest of the Ward's colored men was engaged in cleaning cuspidors or some like avocation. Upon him, without warning, came the hefty piece of feminine avoirdupois prostrating him to the earth. As soon as he could regain breath and feet he ran to the street shouting, "Oh Lawd! Oh Lawd! I'se converted. I is a reformed niggah I is, I is," and never thereafter could he be induced to enter the "Red Lion."

This view of the intersection of State and Filbert Streets in the east end of the Eighth looks south down Filbert, past South, to Walnut Street. (HSDC)

34. How the "Red Lion" Entertained

July 7, 1913

Perchance, some reader may say "a great amount of space is being given to 'the Red Lion.' " I am taking "the Red Lion" as typical of a flagrant form of vice which long flourished, substantially unmolested, in portions of the "Old Eighth," because I want to draw a moral and a lesson as to civic responsibility for conditions so gross. Not all the houses of the class to which the Red Lion belonged were quite as brazen and defiant of external appearances as it was; but in all there was the same heartlessness, the same selfish disregard of the rights of others or the dictates of right, the same plotting to ruin bodies and souls for sordid gain.

A Specimen "Red Lion" Scrap

As numerous are the tales handed down by tradition of more or less bloody encounters at the "Red Lion," for, without at least one fight a day, it would not have appeared to be in its normal atmosphere. One only will be presented, of a character unique even in tenderloin scraps.

It is drawn from the recollection of an aged and worthy citizen who once sowed some wild oats, just to see what the crop would be. In a few years he did not find the reaping at all satisfactory and eschewed that line of agricultural industry.

One balmy day about 40 summers ago, there came to the city three toughs from an up-river location. Two, of medium size, were a little dubious about the ability of the two [missing line] . . . satisfactory the whole town of Harrisburg which they had heard was a fairly tough place.

The third, a riverman of gigantic size, who had assumed the leadership of the party, assured the doubters that wherever he went, it was a "veni, vidi, vici" affair, and that he would lead them to victory. After various libations, the three entered the "Red Lion," the captain boldly announcing that he was a sure-enough sport from up Williamsport way, and that he could whip a ton of wild-cats before breakfast.

He drank at the bar; he ogled and treated the females of the ranch, and scowled ominously at the males as an intimation of what might be expected if any one trod on his coins, he ambled through the house—and he met his Waterloo. And that Waterloo happened thus: On a second floor landing he encountered a female that he deemed needed some correction, and he was not the man to shirk duty when it came to slapping a woman.

The assaulted one gave a shriek of pain and terror; and there was a prompt answering yell that possessed neither pain nor terror, for the landlord's wife, far down the narrow hallway, had seen the performance, and was quite as ready for a little rough and tumble sport as was the tough from up Williamsport way. The yell she emitted was about as shrill and blood-curdling as an Indian war whoop and the "haroof" battle cry of Dan Rice's circus men combined.

One of those huge hickory mops of the olden time was close at hand. The Amazonian of the Red Lion wanted no better weapon; and, a moment later, it was playing a tattoo on the tough's skull, such as that skull had never experienced before. The up-river sport grasped the rudiments of the situation with an alacrity that was surprising, and sought to descend the stairs. But the war whoop had been the signal to the whole house that the fray was on. From every room came females—some lank and wiry, some short and dumpy, some in very attenuated dresses, and some in no dress at all worth specifying.

The Red Lion Hotel and its bar are on the left past the intersection of South and Cowden Streets in this view looking west up South Street toward the capitol. (PSA)

151

This raucous scene could have been used to illustrate Wert's articles, but it was actually part of Herbert Asbury's 1928 book The Gangs of New York.

All centered on the common enemy with the most amazing celerity. As many as could get near enough clutched locks of his black hair or beard with a laudable determination to have the keep-sake token of the interview. When the locks were all appropriated, others entwined their digits in his features; and, with a view to just such a contingency as had now arisen, it was not the fashion with the feminine population of the "Red Lion" to pare the finger nails closely.

How Up-River Visitors Left

It was a moving spectacle. It had more action and motion to it than any reel ever run off in Harrisburg's movies depicting the Balkan war or the battle of Gettysburg. The movement was toward the head of the stairway—a giant in the center howling with pain, the blood trickly from his gashed face. He was a crushed giant—a heart-broken giant. It had been his proud boast that no man had ever whipped him. And now he had taken the count and was down and out before a pack of feminines.

And then a slowly revolving mass came rolling down the stairs which were too narrow to admit of a rapid movement of that aggregation of humanity. In its progress towards the bar room, legs, arms, heads of disheveled hair of all hues from golden to jet, stockings, slippers, torn skirts, remnants of back combs, hands, feet, and miscellaneous articles of rent apparel were all in evidence. Curses and cries of various kinds came from the conglomerate human ball, no individual member of which could separate himself or herself from the mass; but above all rose the howl of agony from the erstwhile captain of the toughs who now bore the lacerations of more female finger nails than he had inches in his height.

His two companions below—took one look at the free panorama, borrowed a leaf from the book of wisdom, and lit out with as much dispatch as a jack rabbit. A few minutes later they were crossing the Camp Curtin site with their noses set Fort Hunter direction. For aught I ever learned to the contrary, they may be running yet.

When the fracas burst forth some one called the landlord's attention to it. He looked up the stairway a moment, remarked carelessly, "I see the old 'ooman is there. I guess the galoot will git all that's comin' to him." He now, however, assumed the role of Good Samaritan by extricating the gentleman from up Williamsport way from the mass of femininity before they could get their hooks in on what little hair his head still retained, and speeding him into the street with a couple of vigorous kicks as souvenirs of his visit to Harrisburg's tenderloin.

The battered remnants of the Lycoming county sport were courtplastered by an obliging druggist of the vicinage who also, for a pecuniary consideration, furnished the victim of misplaced confidence in his own prowess with enough John Barleycorn to drown his sorrow effectually.

A Couch for the Weary

There were many frame buildings at that time on East State street, in front of which were wooden cellar doors almost level with the pavement. On one of these the vanquished giant gracefully stretched himself out and sweetly slumbered the hours away till fell the shades of evening. The sun poured down its rays on his battle-scarred face; the small boy jeered him, when he answered not, gained sufficient courage to prod him with sticks or shower sand on his head; the citizen, as he passed and repassed, remarked that it was a "blankety-blank shame, so it was, that a carcass like that should lumber up the sidewalk all day. What the darnation were the police for anyway, if the people along East State street could have no protection from the miscellaneous hoodlums that the tenderloin drew to it as a street lamp draws gnats and midges?" But through it all the humiliated riverman, who could whip a ton of wild-cats, but had been vanquished ingloriously by feminine finger nails, slept on.

Disgusting exhibitions of a similar character were by no means uncommon on East State street of that period. Forty years ago the police force of Harrisburg was small in number. Its members were poorly paid, blamed for almost everything, thanked for nothing. If a single member of the force wandered up in the tenderloin he was likely to run into trouble with no assurance that he would come off victor, for the toughs who frequented Canal street dearly loved to double team a cop. If he did pick up a drunk too far gone to walk, the only way of removing him to jail was to borrow a wheelbarrow from a grocer and himself furnish the motive power for propelling the monocycle. So it was only human nature to not be very acute in hunting out such jobs for themselves.

35. "Birds of Prey"

July 14, 1913

There are always causes for the existence of tenderloins of which the old "Red Lion" was a type. These causes are a complex combination of many facts. In the recent crusades against and investigations upon what has been euphemistically termed "white slavery," there has been a deal of verbiage and not from well meaning excitable persons, mingled with some very effective action on the part of practical workers. It is not my mission in these articles to separate the wheat from the chaff.

But there was one important factor in the maintenance of the "Old Eighth's" tenderloin, as of every other tenderloin, that afforded a firm foundation for vice.

Uproot it and big strides have been made in the solution of the problem. Many of the Eighth Ward dens were located in buildings owned by reputable members of the community, in some cases pillars in the church. They got all the money they could get for dilapidated shacks, but if asked aught about the character of the tenants, ignored it with a lordly wave of the hand—"They knew naught about the people; the rent was regularly paid; it was not their business to investigate the moral status of their tenants."

Sometimes to absolve themselves from all direct contact with the transaction, an agent was employed—and the only thing that agent had to do was to bring in the money.

Thus the depraved men and women who kept these Eighth Ward dens paid enormous rents—rents which no laboring man or legitimate business could have paid, were obliged to make all necessary repairs themselves; and, naturally, levied toll on all the weak and vicious whom they could enmesh within their nets to recoup their own purses.

Then, while the respectable landlords flourished like green bay trees, bought more old shacks as an investment, and thanked the Lord that was prospering them financially, their wives and daughters dressed gorgeously and mingled in refined society, and yet there were tears and tragedies woven into the wool of each rare fabric they wore.

The men who owned these tenements and coined money from human degradation were wrought to righteous wrath if anyone pressed the subject home too closely. "There might be vice conditions in the Eighth. There were some vile people in this world. They, however, knew naught of them and had no wish to know."

And that is the attitude upon the part of the pillars of society that the devil dearly loves, for it is then that he can reap a prolific harvest, and hold a processional march of triumph over crushed hearts and blasted lives.

"A Bird of Prey"

But the inhabitants of houses like the "Red Lion" were not the only or the most dangerous birds of prey that could be found in the "Old Eighth," for in these vice was in so gross a form that it often repelled instead of allured, the intended victim.

Once on a time, a very attractive woman located in a rather quiet and respectable section of the Ward. A neat sign informed the passerby that boarders and lodgers could find accommodation within. A bachelor business man of the burg was soon found to be deeply interested in the charmer within the mansion. Together the twain—and a right handsome pair they were—visited the carpet stores and the furniture stores, the upholsterer, and the wall paper artisan, until that house was a very dream of beauty within. Even the cupboard was stocked with the choicest wines and liquors.

And then that hard-struck Harrisburg bachelor confided to his friends what a beautiful sweetheart he had caged away from the gaze of the obtrusive world—how true and loyal she was to him—and that whole line of talk that silly men get off. Mayhap, you have some time heard one of the easy marks, reeling off a similar line of conversation.

But there were some amongst the bachelor's friends who were men of the world, and their faces were wreathed with cynical smiles, but the love-lorn one saw it not. They had a right to smile, for this bachelor's peerless Donna Dulcinea had his business hours down fine, and, at such times, there was a miscellaneous line of callers. One in particular lolled in the plush rockers and drank the choice wines and liquors with a frequency that seemed to mark him as an especial favorite.

The Saturday's marketing to furnish the wherewithal for the Sunday feast of which the bachelor always partook with his sweetheart was a gala occasion. It was the special farce in the whole comic performance. Of course the woman in the case felt in duty bound to patronize her lover's grocery store and he always obsequiously waited on her himself. When the basket had been well filled she would ostentatiously pass over a five or a ten dollar bill and the proprietor, with much juggling and show of making change, would pass back the same amount, or even more, in money of other denominations.

The other member of the firm, for it was a partnership concern, began to wonder why the cash drawer each day became leaner and leaner, but I do not

155

think he ever grew fully wise till the inevitable bankruptcy came. And then a lot of people made the usual exclamations of wonder—"How does it come that Blank & Blank failed? They always seemed to be doing a big business."

A Crushed Bachelor

And then the bachelor hied him to the Eighth Ward and told his sweetheart all. He was ruined financially but he would not give up. They would be married, go to a new place and start life over again. He could get something to do.

But she spoke him words of scorning. She never cared a picayune for him except as he was able to produce the coin. If his money was gone, that settled it. Love's dream was all off.

What previous wrongs the siren may have had that had calloused her heart I know not. She may have been the victim of man's baseness who was taking her own way of evening things up.

Another Turn of the Wheel

In the trial of the notorious Jack Johnson case in Chicago, Belle Schreiber testified—"I don't know what love is. I don't believe I had any affection for Johnson. The reasons I associated with him were mostly financial—because I could get lots of clothes and some jewelry from him."

The woman, however, in this case does not appear to have been so utterly destitute of feelings of affection, for she had victimized the bachelor grocer because she loved the star loafer who lolled in the plush rockers and drank the choice wines. They were promptly married. She drew out the tidy bank account which had been accumulated at the expense of a bankrupt firm, and sold off all the furniture on which the bachelor business man had expended funds so lavishly, because the new husband told her of a splendid business opening in the town of York which would make them both millionaires in short order.

To the bustling town of York they went. The husband with all the funds in his pocket, started out to conclude the business deal. His steps happened to turn in the direction of the N.C. station just as a train was pulling out, and she saw him nevermore.

The woman had never heard, probably, of retributive justice, but she felt its sting all the same, and bewailed loudly all the way in which she had been robbed of the money which she had squeezed out of another—then drifted to Raborg street, Baltimore, and, doubtless long since, to an unknown grave over which no mourner shed a tear.

I have told one story associated with a rather neat Eighth Ward dwelling which will soon disappear. It is only one of many, for life in the "Old Eighth" has abounded with funny propositions.

BIBLIOGRAPHY

PRIMARY SOURCES

J. Howard Wert's 35 articles, unsourced, were originally published in the Harrisburg *Patriot* under his byline, beginning on November 18, 1912 and ending on July 14, 1913. They appeared in column form, nearly always on page 4 or 6, under the title "Passing of the Old Eighth" in quotation marks.

SECONDARY SOURCES

Anbinder, Tyler. *Five Points: The 19th-Century New York City Neighborhood That Invented Tap Dance, Stole Elections, and Became the World's Most Notorious Slum.* New York: Free Press, 2000.

Anderson, Benedict. *Imagined Communities.* Rev. ed. New York: Verso, 1991.

Asbury, Herbert. *The Gangs of New York: An Informal History of the Underworld.* New York: Alfred A. Knopf, 1928.

Barton, Michael. *Life by the Moving Road; An Illustrated History of Greater Harrisburg,* 2nd ed. Sun Valley, CA: American Historical Press, 1998.

Bates, Samuel P. *History of Pennsylvania Volunteers, 1861–5.* Vol. 5. Harrisburg: B. Singerly, State Printer, 1871.

Bazelon, Bruce, and George Friedman. *Chisuk Emuna: Strength of Faith.* Harrisburg: Capitol Press, 1984.

Beers, Paul. *Profiles from the Susquehanna Valley.* Harrisburg: Stackpole Books, 1973.

Bradley, Mary O. "Harrisburg Club Catered to Wealthy," (Harrisburg) *Patriot,* September 29, 1998, page D1.

Eggert, Gerald G. *Harrisburg Industrializes; The Coming of Factories to an American Community.* University Park: The Pennsylvania State University Press, 1993.

Hartman, Seymour. "History of the Kesher Israel Congregation," in *Dedication Book; Kesher Israel Synagogue* (Harrisburg: Privately printed, 1949), pp. 9–16.

Hofstadter, Richard. *The Age of Reform.* New York: Vintage, 1955.

Miller, William J. *Civil War City; Harrisburg, Pennsylvania, 1861–1865, the Training of an Army.* Shippensburg: White Mane Publishing Co., Inc., 1990.

Morrison, Ernest. *J. Horace McFarland; A Thorn for Beauty*. Harrisburg: Pennsylvania Historical and Museum Commission, 1995.

Reynolds, David. *Beneath the American Renaissance*. Cambridge: Harvard University Press, 1989.

Steinmetz, Richard H. Sr., and Hoffsommer, Robert D. *This Was Harrisburg; A Photographic History*. Harrisburg: Stackpole Books, 1976.

Wert, J. Howard. *A Complete Hand-book of the Monuments and Indications and Guide to the Positions on the Gettysburg Battlefield*. Harrisburg: R.M. Sturgeon & Co., 1886.

———. *Annals of the Boy's High School of Harrisburg, 1875–1893*. Harrisburg: J. Horace McFarland Co., Mt. Pleasant Printery, 1895.

Wilson, William H. *The City Beautiful Movement*. Baltimore: The Johns Hopkins University Press, 1989.

PHOTOGRAPHS AND OTHER IMAGES

The photographs used in this publication came from two main archives: The Historical Society of Dauphin County and the Pennsylvania State Archives, both in Harrisburg, Pennsylvania. At the Historical Society, an album containing photographs of the Eighth Ward was the main source.

At the Pennsylvania State Archives, the major source of photographs was RG-17, Records of the Department of Land Records. A collection of 76 additional Eighth Ward photographs, taken by Horace McFarland in 1904, 1909, and 1917, is also contained in MG-85, The McFarland Collection.

The press clippings were taken from a bound volume of the Harrisburg *Telegraph* newspaper, covering January to June, 1902, in the possession of Professor Barton.

INDEX